CHRIST A COMPLETE SAVIOUR

CHRIST

A COMPLETE SAVIOUR

THE INTERCESSION OF CHRIST,

AND WHO ARE PRIVILEGED IN IT

BY

JOHN BUNYAN

MINNEAPOLIS
2012

Published by Curiosmith.
P. O. Box 390293, Minneapolis, Minnesota, 55439.
Internet: curiosmith.com.
E-mail: shopkeeper@curiosmith.com.

Previously published in 1692 by E. Chandler, J. Wilson, and C. Doe.

The "Outline of the Contents" was added to this edition by the publisher.

ISBN 9781935626190

OUTLINE OF THE CONTENTS

————•◇•————

(Continued on the next page.)

(Continued on the next page.)

ADVERTISEMENT

However strange it may appear, it is a solemn fact, that the heart of man, unless prepared by a sense of the exceeding sinfulness of sin, rejects Christ as a complete Saviour. The pride of human nature will not suffer it to fall, as helpless and utterly undone, into the arms of Divine mercy. Man prefers a partial Saviour; one who had done so much, that, *with the sinner's aid*, the work might be completed. Not such were the opinions of John Bunyan; the furnace of sharp conviction had burnt up this proud dross; he believed the testimony of Scripture, that from the crown of the head to the soles of the feet all nature is corrupted; so that out of the unsanctified heart of man proceed evil thoughts, murders, and the sad catalogue of crimes which our Lord enumerates, and which defile our best efforts after purity of heart and life. No sinner will ever totally rely upon the Saviour until he is sensible of his own perishing state; hanging by the brittle thread of life over the yawning gulf of perdition; sinking in that sin which will swallow him up in those awful torments which await the transgressor; feeling that sin has fitted him as stubble for the fire; then it is that the cry proceeds from his heart, Lord, save, I perish; and then, and not till then, are we made willing to receive 'Christ as a complete Saviour' to the uttermost, not of his ability, but of our necessity. This was the subject of all Mr. Bunyan's writings, and, doubtless, of all his preaching. It was to direct sinners to the Lamb of God, who alone can take away sin. This little treatise was one of those ten 'excellent manuscripts' which, at Bunyan's decease, were found prepared for the press.

It was first published in 1692, by his friends E. Chandler, J. Wilson, and C. Doe.

It is limited to a subject which is too often lost sight of, because it is within the veil—the intercession of Christ as the finishing work of a sinner's salvation. Many persons limit the 'looking unto Jesus' to beholding him upon the cross, a common popish error; but this is not enough; we must, in our minds, follow him to the unseen world, and thus ascend to a risen Saviour, at the right hand of the Father, making intercession for our daily sins. And he is our ONLY Intercessor, and it is a rejection of him, for us to seek the aid of another. Who ever was mad enough to ask Moses to intercede for him, and surely he is as able as Mary or any other saint? To atone for sin calls for the amazing price of the blood of Christ, who was 'God manifest in the flesh.' He undertook the work by covenant; and all the 'saved' form part of his mystical body; thus perfectly obeying the law in him. He poured out his life to open a fountain for sin and uncleanness; and as they are liable to pollution in their passage through the world, he only is able, and he ever liveth, to make intercession for their transgressions. Thus he becomes a complete Saviour, and will crown, with an eternal weight of glory, all those that put their trust in him. Beautiful, and soul-softening, and heartwarming thoughts abound in this little work, which cannot fail to make a lasting impression upon the reader. Bunyan disclaims 'the beggarly art of complimenting' in things of such solemnity, PAGE 42. He describes the heart as *unweldable*, a remarkable expression, drawn from his father's trade of a blacksmith; nothing but grace can so heat it as to enable the hammer of conviction to weld it to Christ; and when thus welded, it becomes one with him, PAGE 50. There is hope for a returning backslider in a complete Saviour; he combines the evidence of two men, the coming and the returning sinner; he has been, like Jonah, in the belly of hell; his sins, like talking devils, have driven him back to the Saviour. Sin brings its own punishment, from which we escape by keeping in the narrow path. Good works save us from temporal miseries, which ever follow an indulgence in sin; but if we fall, we have an Advocate and

Intercessor to lift us up; still, if thou lovest thy soul, slight not the knowledge of hell, for that, with the law, are the spurs which Christ useth to prick souls forward to himself. O gather up thy heels and mend thy pace, or those spurs will be in thy sides, PAGE 61. Take heed, O persecutor; like Saul, thou art exceeding mad, and hell is thy bedlam. Take heed of a false faith; none is true but that which is acquired by a *kneeling*, searching, seeking for truth as for hid treasure. Death is God's bailiff, he will seize thee without warning; but with the saints, the grave's mouth is the final parting place between grace and sin, PAGE 104. Forget not that a good improvement will make your little grace to thrive, PAGE 111. Reader, may Divine grace indelibly fix these wholesome truths upon our minds.

GEORGE OFFOR

INTRODUCTION

Wherefore he is able also to save them to the uttermost that come unto God by him, seeing he ever liveth to make intercession for them.—HEBREWS 7:25.

THE apostle, in this chapter, presenteth us with two things; that is, with the greatness of the person and of the priesthood of our Lord Jesus.

First, He presenteth us with the greatness of his person, in that he preferreth him before Abraham, who is the father of us all; yea, in that he preferreth him before Melchisedec, who was above Abraham, and blessed him who had the promises.

Second, As to his priesthood, he showeth the greatness of that, in that he was made a priest, not by the law of a carnal commandment, but by the power of an endless life. Not without, but with an oath, by him that said, 'The Lord sware, and will not repent, Thou *art* a priest for ever, after the order of Melchisedec;' wherefore, 'this *man*, because he continueth ever, hath an unchangeable priesthood.' Now my text is drawn from this conclusion, namely, that Christ abideth a priest continually. 'Wherefore he is able also to save them to the uttermost that come unto God by him, seeing he ever liveth to make intercession for them.'

In the words, I take notice of four things:

FIRST, Of the intercession of Christ—He maketh intercession.

SECOND, Of the benefit of his intercession—'Wherefore he is able to save to the uttermost,' etc.

THIRD, We have also here set before us the persons interested in this intercession of Christ—And they are those 'that come unto God by him.'

FOURTH, We have also here the certainty of their reaping this benefit by him; to wit, seeing he ever liveth to make intercession for them—'Wherefore he is able also to save them to the uttermost that come unto God by him, seeing he ever liveth to make intercession for them.'[1]

---

1 Coming unto God by Christ, essentially involves in it walking in conformity to his image; and all such comers must be perfectly and eternally saved. Why then, O child of God, should you suffer under Giant Despair, in his doubting, fearing castle.—OFFOR.

CHAPTER I

THE INTERCESSION OF CHRIST

First, We will begin with HIS INTERCESSION, and will show you, *First*, What that is; *Second*, For what he intercedes; and, *Third*, What is also to be inferred from Christ's making intercession for us.

First, I begin, then, with the first; that is, to show you *what intercession is*. Intercession is prayer; but all prayer is not intercession. Intercession, then, is that prayer that is made by a third person about the concerns that are between two. And it may be made either to set them at further difference, or to make them friends; for intercession may be made against, as well as for, a person or people. 'Wot ye not what the Scripture saith of Elias? how he maketh intercession to God against Israel.'[1] But the intercession that we are now to speak of is not an intercession of this kind, not an intercession against, but an intercession for a people. 'He ever liveth to make intercession for them.' The high priest is ordained for, but not to be against the people. 'Every high priest taken from among men is ordained for men in things *pertaining* to God,' to make reconciliation for the sins of the people; or 'that he may offer both gifts and sacrifices for sins.'[2] This, then, is intercession; and the intercession of Christ is to be between two, between God and man, for man's good. And it extendeth itself unto these:

1. To pray that the elect may be brought all home to him; that is, to God.

---

1 Romans 11:2.
2 Hebrews 5:1.

2. To pray that their sins committed after conversion may be forgiven them.

3. To pray that their graces which they receive at conversion may be maintained and supplied.

4. To pray that their persons may be preserved unto his heavenly kingdom.

Second, This is the intercession of Christ, or *that for which he doth make intercession.*

1. He prays for all the elect, that they may be brought home to God, and so into the unity of the faith, etc. This is clear, for that he saith, 'Neither pray I for these alone;' that is, for those only that are converted; 'but for them also which shall believe on me through their word;' for all them that shall, that are appointed to believe; or, as you have it a little above, 'for them which thou hast given me.'[1] And the reason is, for that he hath paid a ransom for them. Christ, therefore, when he maketh intercession for the ungodly, and all the unconverted elect are such, doth but petitionarily ask for his own, his purchased ones, those for whom he died before, that they might be saved by his blood.

2. When any of them are brought home to God, he yet prays for them; namely, that the sins which through infirmity they, after conversion, may commit, may also be forgiven them.

This is showed us by the intercession of the high priest under the law, that was to bear away the iniquities of the holy things of the children of Israel; yea, and also by his atonement for them that sinned; for that it saith, 'And the priest shall make an atonement for him, for his sin which he hath sinned, and it shall be forgiven him.'[2] This also is intimated even where our Lord doth make intercession, saying, 'I pray not that thou shouldest take them out of the world, but that thou shouldest keep them from the evil.'[3] That Christ prayed that the converted should be kept from all manner of commission of sin, must not be supposed, for that is the way to make his intercession, at

---

1 John 17:9, 20; Isaiah 53:12.
2 Leviticus 5:10.
3 John 17:15.

least in some things, invalid, and to contradict himself; for, saith he, 'I know that thou hearest me always.'[1] But the meaning is, I pray that thou wouldest keep them from soul-damning delusions, such as are unavoidably such; also that thou wouldest keep them from the soul-destroying evil of every sin, of every temptation. Now this he doth by his prevailing and by his pardoning grace.

3. In his intercession he prayeth also that those graces which we receive at conversion may be maintained and supplied. This is clear where he saith, 'Simon, Simon, behold, Satan hath desired *to have* you, that he may sift *you* as wheat; but I have prayed for thee, that thy faith fail not.'[2] Ay, may some say, he is said to pray here for the support and supply of faith, but doth it therefore follow that he prayed for the maintaining and supply of all our graces? Yes, in that he prayed for the preservation of our faith, he prayed for the preservation of all our graces; for faith is the mother grace, the root grace, the grace that hath all others in the bowels of it, and that from the which all others flow; yea, it is that which gives being to all our other graces, and that by which all the rest do live. Let, then, faith be preserved, and all graces continue and live—that is, according to the present state, health, and degree of faith. So, then, Christ prayed for the preservation of every grace when he prayed for the preservation of faith. That text also is of the same tendency where he saith, 'Keep through thine own name those whom thou hast given me.'[3] Keep them in thy fear, in the faith, in the true religion, in the way of life by thy grace, by thy power, by thy wisdom, etc. This must be much of the meaning of this place, and he that excludes this sense will make but poor work of another exposition.

4. He also in his intercession prayeth that our persons be preserved, and brought safe unto his heavenly kingdom. And this he doth, (1.) By pleading interest in them. (2.) By pleading that he had given, by promise, glory to them. (3.) By pleading his own resolution to have it so. (4.) By pleading the reason why it must be so.

---

1 John 11:42.
2 Luke 22:31–32.
3 John 17:11.

(1.) He prays that their persons may come to glory, for that they are his, and that by the best of titles: 'Thine they were, and thou gavest them me.'[1] Father, I will have them; Father, I will have them, for they are mine: 'Thine they were, and thou gavest them me.' What is mine, my wife, or my child, or my jewel, or my joy, sure I may have it with me. Thus, therefore, he pleads or cries in his intercession, that our persons might be preserved to glory: They are mine, 'and thou gavest them me.'[2]

(2.) He also pleads that he had given—given already, that is, in the promise—glory to them, and therefore they must not go without it. 'And the glory which thou gavest me I have given them.'[3] Righteous men, when they give a good thing by promise, they design the performance of that promise; nay, they more than design it, they purpose, they determine it. As the mad prophet also saith of God, in another case, 'Hath he said, and shall he not do *it*? or hath he spoken, and shall he not make it good?'[4] Hath Christ given us glory, and shall we not have it? Yea, hath the truth itself bestowed it upon us, and shall those to whom it is given, even given by Scripture of truth, be yet deprived thereof?

(3.) He pleads in his interceding that they might have glory; his own resolution to have it so. 'Father, I will that they also, whom thou hast given me, be with me where I am.'[5] Behold ye here, he is resolved to have it so. It must be so. It shall be so. I will have it so. We read of Adonijah, that his father never denied him in anything. He never said to him, 'Why hast thou done so?'[6] Indeed, he denied him the kingdom; for his brother was heir of that from the Lord. How much more will our Father let our Lord Jesus have his mind and will in this, since

---

1 John 17:6.
2 What indescribable consolations flow into the Christian's soul from communion with God, especially to the most deeply afflicted. Thus the widow casts her care upon her heavenly Father—her Creator, Christ; for all things were made by him. He is her husband, ever living to intercede for her. Wondrous privileges!—OFFOR.
3 John 17:22.
4 Numbers 23:19.
5 John 17:24.
6 1 Kings 1:6.

he also is as willing to have it so as is the Son himself. 'Fear not, little flock; for it is your Father's good pleasure to give you the kingdom.'[1] Resolution will drive things far, especially resolution to do that which none but they that cannot hinder shall oppose. Why this is the case, the resolution of our Intercessor is, that we be preserved to glory; yea, and this resolution he pleads in his intercession: 'Father, I will that they also, whom thou hast given me, be with me where I am,' etc.[2] Must it not, therefore, now be so?

(4.) He also, in the last place, in this his intercession, urges a reason why he will have it so, namely, 'That they may behold my glory, which thou hast given me; for thou lovedst me before the foundation of the world,' verse 24. And this is a reason to the purpose; it is as if he had said, Father, these have continued with me in my temptations; these have seen me under all my disadvantages; these have seen me in my poor, low, contemptible condition; these have seen what scorn, reproach, slanders, and disgrace I have borne for thy sake in the world; and now I will have them also be where they shall see me in my glory. I have told them that I am thy Son, and they have believed that; I have told them that thou lovest me, and they have believed that; I have also told them that thou wouldest take me again to glory, and they have believed that; but they have not seen my glory, nor can they but be like the Queen of Sheba, they will but believe by the halves unless their own eyes do behold it. Besides, Father, these are they that love me, and it will be an increase of their joy if they may but see me in glory; it will be as a heaven to their hearts to see their Saviour in glory. I will, therefore, that those which 'thou hast given me be with me where I am, that they may behold my glory.' This, therefore, is a reason why Christ Jesus our Lord intercedes to have his people with him in glory.

Third, I come now to the third thing, namely, to show you *what is to be inferred from Christ's making intercession for us.*

1. This is to be inferred from hence, that saints—for I will here

1 Luke 12:32.
2 John 17:24.

say nothing of those of the elect uncalled—do ofttimes give occasion of offence to God, even they that have received grace; for intercession is made to continue one in the favour of another, and to make up those breaches that, at any time, shall happen to be made by one to the alienating of the affections of the other. And thus he makes reconciliation for iniquity; for reconciliation may be made for iniquity two ways: first, by paying of a price; secondly, by insisting upon the price paid for the offender by way of intercession. Therefore you read that as the goat was to be killed, so his blood was, by the priest, to be brought within the veil, and, in a way of intercession, to be sprinkled before and upon the mercy-seat: 'Then shall he kill the goat of the sin-offering, that *is*, for the people, and bring his blood within the veil, and do with that blood as he did with the blood of the bullock, and sprinkle it upon the mercy-seat, and before the mercy-seat; and he shall make an atonement for the holy *place*, because of the uncleanness of the children of Israel, and because of their transgressions in all their sins: and so shall he do for the tabernacle of the congregation that remaineth among them, in the midst of their uncleanness.'[1] This was to be done, as you see, that the tabernacle, which was the place of God's presence and graces, might yet remain among the children of Israel, notwithstanding their uncleannesses and transgressions. This, also, is the effect of Christ's intercession; it is that the signs of God's presence and his grace might remain among his people, notwithstanding they have, by their transgressions, so often provoked God to depart from them.

2. By Christ's intercession I gather, that awakened men and women, such as the godly are, dare not, after offence given, come in their own names to make unto God an application for mercy. God, in himself, is a consuming fire, and sin has made the best of us as stubble is to fire; wherefore, they may not, they cannot, they dare not approach God's presence for help but by and through a mediator and intercessor. When Israel saw the fire, the blackness and darkness, and heard the thunder, and lightning, and the terrible sound of the

---

1 Leviticus 16:15–16.

trumpet, 'they said unto Moses, Speak thou with us, and we will hear: but let not God speak with us, lest we die.'[1] Guilt, and sense of the disparity that is betwixt God and us, will make us look out for a man that may lay his hand upon us both, and that may set us right in the eyes of our Father again. This, I say, I infer from the intercession of Christ; for, if there had been a possibility of our ability to have approached God with advantage without, what need had there been of the intercession of Christ?

Absalom durst not approach—no, not the presence of his father—by himself, without a mediator and intercessor; wherefore, he sends to Joab to go to the king and make intercession for him.[2] Also, Joab durst not go upon that errand himself, but by the mediation of another. Sin is a fearful thing, it will quash and quail the courage of a man, and make him afraid to approach the presence of him whom he has offended, though the offended is but a man. How much more, then, shall it discourage a man, when once loaden with guilt and shame, from attempting to approach the presence of a holy and a sin-avenging God, unless he can come to him through, and in the name of, an intercessor? But here now is the help and comfort of the people of God—there is to help them under all their infirmities an intercessor prepared, and at work. 'He ever liveth to make intercession.'

3. I also infer from hence, that should we, out of an ignorant boldness and presumption, attempt, when we have offended, by ourselves to approach the presence of God, God would not accept us. He told Eliphaz so. What Eliphaz thought, or was about to do, I know not; but God said unto him, 'My wrath is kindled against thee, and against thy two friends; for ye have not spoken of me *the thing that is* right, as my servant Job *hath*. Therefore take unto you now seven bullocks, and seven rams, and go to my servant Job, and offer up for yourselves (that is, by him) a burnt-offering, and my servant Job shall pray for you; for him will I accept; lest I deal with you *after your*

1 Exodus 20:19; Deuteronomy 18:16.
2 2 Samuel 13; 14:32–33.

folly, in that ye have not spoken of me *the thing which is* right, like my servant Job.' See here, an offence is a bar and an obstruction to acceptance with God, but by a mediator, but by an intercessor. He that comes to God by himself, God will answer him by himself—that is, without an intercessor; and I will tell you, such are not like to get any pleasant or comfortable answer—I will answer him that so cometh according to the multitude of his idols. 'And I will set my face against that man, and will make him a sign and a proverb, and I will cut him off from the midst of my people; and ye shall know that I *am* the Lord.'[1]

He that intercedes for another with a holy and just God had need be clean himself, lest he with whom he so busieth himself say to him, First clear thyself, and then come and speak for thy friend. Wherefore, this is the very description and qualification of this our High Priest and blessed Intercessor, 'For such an high priest became us, *who is* holy, harmless, undefiled, separate from sinners, and made higher than the heavens; who needeth not daily, as those high priests, to offer up sacrifice, first for his own sins,' etc.[2] Had we not had such an Intercessor, we had been but in a very poor case; but we have one that becomes us; one that fits us to the purpose; one against whom our God hath nothing, can object nothing; one in whose mouth no guile could be found.[3]

4. Since Christ is an Intercessor, I infer that he has wherewithal in readiness to answer to any demands that may be propounded by him that hath been by us offended, in order to a renewing of peace and letting out of that grace to us that we have sinned away, and yet have need of. Ofttimes the offended saith to the intercessor, Well, thou comest to me about this man; what interest he has in thee is one thing, what offence he has committed against me is another. I

---

1 Ezekiel 14:7–8.
2 Hebrews 7:26–27.
3 The infinite perfection of the Mediatorial work of Jesus, God manifest in the flesh, is the ground of our hope. He alone can effectually plead with God. O my soul! if, in thy holiest and happiest moments, thou art found 'looking unto Jesus,' how much more intensely ought thy trembling eye to be directed to him, when thou art wounded by sin!!—OFFOR.

speak now after the manner of men. Now, what can an intercessor do, if he is not able to answer this question? But now, if he be able to answer this question—that is, according to law and justice, no question but he may prevail with the offended, for him for whom he makes intercession.

Why, this is our case; to be sure, thus far it is, we have offended a just and a holy God, and Jesus Christ is become Intercessor. He also knows full well, that for our parts, if it would save us from hell, we cannot produce towards a peace with God so much as poor two farthings; that is, not anything that can by law and justice be esteemed worth a halfpenny; yet he makes intercession. It follows, therefore, that he has wherewith of his own, if that question afore is propounded, to answer to every reasonable demand. Hence, it is said, that he has gifts as well as sacrifice for sin. 'Every high priest is ordained to offer gifts and sacrifices: wherefore *it is* of necessity that this man have somewhat also to offer.'[1] And, observe it, the apostle speaks here of Christ as in heaven, there ministering in the second part of his office; 'For if he were on earth, he should not be a priest.' verse 4. These gifts, therefore, and this sacrifice, he now offereth in heaven by way of intercession, urging and pleading as an Intercessor, the valuableness of his gifts for the pacifying of that wrath that our Father hath conceived against us for the disobediences that we are guilty of. 'A gift in secret pacifieth anger; and a reward in the bosom strong wrath.'[2]

What gifts these are the Scripture everywhere testifies. He gave himself, he gave his life, he gave his all for us.[3] These gifts, as he offered them up at the demand of justice on Mount Calvary for us, so now he is in heaven he presenteth them continually before God, as gifts and sacrifice valuable for the sins, for all the sins that we, through infirmity, do commit, from the day of our conversion to the day of our death. And these gifts are so satisfactory, so prevalent with

1 Hebrews 8:3.
2 Proverbs 21:14.
3 John 6; Galatians 1:4; 1 Timothy 2:6; Matthew 20:28.

God, that they always prevail for a continual remission of our sins with him. Yea, they prevail with him for more than for the remission of sins; we have, through their procurement, our graces often renewed, the devil often rebuked, the snare often broken, guilt often taken away from the conscience, and many a blessed smile from God, and love-look from his life-creating countenance.[1]

5. Since Christ is an Intercessor, I infer that believers should not rest at the cross for comfort; justification they should look for there; but, being justified by his blood, they should ascend up after him to the throne. At the cross you will see him in his sorrows and humiliations, in his tears and blood; but follow him to where he is now, and then you shall see him in his robes, in his priestly robes, and with his golden girdle about his paps. Then you shall see him wearing the breastplate of judgment, and with all your names written upon his heart. Then you shall perceive that the whole family in heaven and earth is named by him, and how he prevaileth with God the Father of mercies, for you. Stand still awhile and listen; yea, enter with boldness into the holiest, and see your Jesus as he now appears in the presence of God for you; what work he makes against the devil and sin, and death and hell, for you.[2] Ah! it is brave following of Jesus Christ to the holiest, the veil is rent, you may see with open face as in a glass, the glory of the Lord. This, then, is our High Priest, this his intercession, these the benefits of it! It lieth on our part to improve it; and wisdom to do that also comes from the mercy-seat, or throne of grace, where he, even our High Priest, ever liveth to make intercession for us; to whom be glory for ever and ever.

---

1 Ephesians 3:12.
2 Hebrews 10:9.

CHAPTER II

THE BENEFITS OF CHRIST'S INTERCESSION

Second. And thus have I spoken to the first thing—to wit, of the intercession of Christ; and now I come more particularly to speak to the second, THE BENEFITS OF HIS INTERCESSION; namely, that we are saved thereby. Wherefore he is able also to save them, seeing he maketh intercession for them. 'He is able to save them to the uttermost.'

In my handling of this head, I must show you, *First*, What the apostle means here by 'save'—'Wherefore he is able to save.' *Second*, What he means here by saving to the 'uttermost'—'He is able to save to the uttermost.' *Third*, And then, thirdly, we shall do as we did in the foregoing—to wit, gather some inferences from the whole, and speak to them.

WHAT IT MEANS TO 'SAVE'

First, What doth the apostle mean here by '*save*'—'He is able to *save* them.'

To 'save' may be taken two ways. In the general, I know it may be taken many ways, for there are many salvations that we enjoy; yea, that we never knew of, nor can know, until we come thither, where all secret things shall be seen, and where that which has been done in darkness shall be proclaimed upon the housetops. But I say there are two ways that this word may be taken—1. To save in a way of justification. 2. Or to save in a way of preservation. Now, Christ saves both these ways. But which of these, or whether both of them are intended in this place, of that I shall tell you my thoughts anon; meanwhile, I will show you,

1. What it is to be saved in the first sense, [namely, in a way of justification,] and also how that is brought to pass.

To be saved is to be delivered from guilt of sin that is by the law, as it is the ministration of death and condemnation; or, to be set free therefrom before God. This is to be saved; for he that is not set free therefrom, whatever he may think of himself, or whatever others may think concerning him, he is a condemned man. It saith not, he *shall be*, but, he *is* condemned *already*.[1] The reason is, for that he has deserved the sentence of the ministration of condemnation, which is the law. Yea, that law has already arraigned, accused, and condemned him before God, for that it hath found him guilty of sin. Now he that is set free from this, or, as the phrase is, 'being made free from sin,'[2] that is, from the imputation of guilt, there can, to him, be no condemnation, no condemnation to hell fire; but the person thus made free may properly be said to be saved. Wherefore, as sometimes it saith, we *shall* be saved, respecting saving in the second sense, or the utmost completing of salvation; so sometimes it saith, we *are* saved, as respecting our being already secured from guilt, and so from condemnation to hell for sin, and so set safe, and quit from the second death before God.[3]

Now, saving thus comes to us by what Christ did for us in this world, by what Christ did for us as suffering for us. I say, it comes to us thus; that is, it comes to us by grace through the redemption that is in Christ. And thus to be saved is called justification, justification to life, because one thus saved is, as I said, acquitted from guilt, and that everlasting damnation to which for sin he had made himself obnoxious by the law.[4]

Hence we are said to be saved by his death, justified by his blood,

1 John 3:18.
2 Romans 6:22.
3 1 Corinthians 1:18; Ephesians 2:5.
4 1 Corinthians 15:1–4; Romans 5:8–10.

and reconciled to God by the death of his Son; all which must respect his offering of himself on the day he died, and not his improving of his so dying in a way of intercession, because in the same place the apostle reserveth a second, or an additional salvation, and applieth that to his intercession, 'Much more then, being now,' or already, 'justified by his blood, we shall be saved from wrath through him;' that is, through what he will further do for us. 'For if, when we were enemies, we were reconciled to God by the death of his Son, much more, being reconciled,' that is, by his death, 'we shall be saved by his life,' his intercession, which he ever liveth to complete.[1]

See here, we are said to be justified, reconciled already, and therefore we shall be saved, justified by his blood and death, and saved through him by his life.

2. Now the saving intended in the text is saving in this second sense; that is, a saving of us by preserving us, by delivering of us from all those hazards that we run betwixt our state of justification and our state of glorification. Yea, such a saving of us as we that are justified need to bring us into glory. Therefore,

When he saith he is able to save, seeing he ever liveth to make intercession, he addeth saving to saving; saving by his life to saving by his death; saving by his improving of his blood to saving by his spilling of his blood. He gave himself a ransom for us, and now improves that gift in the presence of God by way of intercession. For, as I have hinted already, the high priests under the law took the blood of the sacrifices that were offered for sin, and brought it within the veil, and there sprinkled it before and upon the mercy-seat, and by it made intercession for the people to an additional way of saving them; the sum of which Paul thus applies to Christ when he saith, 'He can save, seeing he ever liveth to make intercession.'

That also in the Romans is clear to this purpose, 'Who *is* he that condemneth? *It is* Christ that died.'[2] That is, who is he that shall lay anything to the charge of God's elect to condemnation to hell, since

---

1 Romans 5:9–10.
2 Romans 8:31–39.

Christ has taken away the curse by his death from before God? Then he adds, that there is nothing that *shall yet* happen to us, shall destroy us, since Christ also liveth to make intercession for us, 'Who shall condemn? *It is* Christ that died; yea, rather, that is risen again, who is even at the right hand of God, who also maketh intercession for us.'

Christ, then, by his death saveth us as we are sinners, enemies, and in a state of condemnation by sin; and Christ by his life saveth us as considered justified, and reconciled to God by his blood. So, then, we have salvation from that condemnation that sin had brought us unto, and salvation from those ruins that all the enemies of our souls would yet bring us unto, but cannot; for the intercession of Christ preventeth.[1,2]

Christ hath redeemed us from the curse of the law. Whatever the law can take hold of to curse us for, that Christ has redeemed us from, by being made a curse for us. But this curse that Christ was made for us, must be confined to his sufferings, not to his exaltation, and, consequently, not to his intercession, for Christ is made no curse but when he suffered; not in his intercession: so then, as he died he took away the curse, and sin that was the cause thereof, by the sacrifice of himself,[3] and by his life, his intercession, he saveth us from all those things that attempt to bring us into that condemnation again.

The salvation, then, that we have by the intercession of Christ, as was said—I speak now of them that are capable of receiving comfort and relief by this doctrine—is salvation that follows upon, or that comes after, justification. We that are saved as to justification of life, need yet to be saved with that that preserveth to glory; for though by the death of Christ we are saved from the curse of the law, yet attempts are made by many that we may be kept from the glory that justified persons are designed for; and from these we are saved by his intercession.

A man, then, that must be eternally saved is to be considered, (*a.*)

---

1 What can withstand the will of Christ, that all his should behold and partake of his glory? He is the Captain of salvation, has subdued all our enemies for us, and will destroy their power in us, and, ere long, put our last enemy, death, under his feet.—Mason.

2 Romans 6:7–10.

3 Galatians 3:13.

As an heir of wrath. (*b.*) As an heir of God. An heir of wrath he is in himself by sin; an heir of God he is by grace through Christ.[1] Now, as an heir of wrath he is redeemed, and as an heir of God he is preserved; as an heir of wrath he is redeemed by blood, and as an heir of God he is preserved by this intercession. Christ by his death, then, puts me, I being reconciled to God thereby, into a justified state, and God accepts me to grace and favour through him. But this doth not hinder but that, all this notwithstanding, there are, that would frustrate me of the end to which I am designed by this reconciliation to God, by redemption through grace; and from the accomplishing of this design I am saved by the blessed intercession of our Lord Jesus Christ.

Objection. 1. Perhaps some may say, we are not saved from all punishment of sin by the death of Christ; and if so, so not from all danger of damnation by the intercession of Christ.

Answer. We are saved from all punishment in hell fire by the death of Christ. Jesus has 'delivered us from the wrath to come.'[2] So that as to this great punishment, God for his sake has forgiven us all trespasses.[3] But we being translated from being slaves to Satan to be sons of God, God reserveth yet this liberty in his hand to chastise us if we offend, as a father chastiseth his son.[4] But this chastisement is not in legal wrath, but in fatherly affection; not to destroy us, but that still we might be made to get advantage thereby, even be made partakers of his holiness. This is, that we might 'not be condemned with the world.'[5] As to the second part of the objection; there do, as we say, many things happen betwixt or between the cup and the lip; many things attempt to overthrow the work of God, and to cause that we should perish through our weakness, notwithstanding the price that hath by Christ been paid for us. But what saith the Scripture? 'Who shall separate us from the love of Christ? *shall* tribulation, or distress, or persecution, or famine, or nakedness, or peril, or sword? As it is

---

1 Ephesians 2:3; Galatians 4:7.
2 1 Thessalonians 1:10.
3 Colossians 2:13.
4 Deuteronomy 8:5.
5 Hebrews 12:5–11; 1 Corinthians 11:32.

written, For thy sake we are killed all the day long; we are accounted as sheep for the slaughter. Nay, in all these things we are more than conquerors through him that loved us. For I am persuaded, that neither death, nor life, nor angels, nor principalities, nor powers, nor things present, nor things to come, nor height, nor depth, nor any other creature, shall be able to separate us from the love of God, which is in Christ Jesus our Lord.'[1]

Thus the apostle reckoneth up all the disadvantages that a justified person is incident to in this life, and by way of challenge declares, that not any one of them, nor all together, shall be able to separate us from the love of God, that is towards us by Christ, his death, and his intercession.

Objection 2. It may be further objected, that the apostle doth here leave out sin, unto which we know the saints are subject, after justification. And sin of itself, we need no other enemies, is of that nature as to destroy the whole world.

Answer. Sin is sin, in the nature of sin, wherever it is found. But sin as to the damning effects thereof is taken away from them unto whom righteousness is imputed for justification. Nor shall any or all the things aforementioned, though there is a tendency in every one of them to drive us unto sin, drown us, through it, in perdition and destruction. I am persuaded, says Paul, they shall never be able to do that. The apostle, therefore, doth implicitly, though not expressly, challenge sin, yea, sin by all its advantages; and then glorieth in the love of God in Christ Jesus, from which he concludeth it shall never separate the justified. Besides, it would now have been needless to have expressly here put in sin by itself, seeing before, he had argued that those he speaks of were freely justified therefrom.

One word more before I go to the second head. The Father, as I told you, has reserved to himself a liberty to chastise his sons, to wit, with temporal chastisements, if they offend. This still abideth to us, notwithstanding God's grace, Christ's death, or blessed intercession. And this punishment is so surely entailed to the transgressions that

---

1 Romans 8:35–39.

we who believe shall commit, that it is impossible that we should be utterly freed therefrom; insomuch that the apostle positively concludeth them to be bastards, what pretences to sonship soever they have, that are not, for sin, partakers of fatherly chastisements.

For the reversing of this punishment it is that we should pray, if perhaps God will remit it, when we are taught to say, 'Our Father, forgive us our trespasses.' And he that admits of any other sense as to this petition, derogates from the death of Christ, or faith, or both. For either he concludes that for some of his sins Christ did not die, or that he is bound to believe that God, though he did, has not yet, nor will forgive them, till from the petitioner some legal work be done; forgive us, as we forgive them that trespass against us.[1] But now, apply this to temporal punishments, and then it is true that God has reserved a liberty in his hand to punish even the sins of his people upon them; yea, and will not pardon their sin, as to the remitting of such punishment, unless some good work by them be done; 'If ye forgive not men their trespasses, neither will your Father forgive your trespasses.'[2]

And this is the cause why some that belong to God are yet so under the afflicting hand of God; they have sinned, and God, who is their Father, punisheth; yea, and this is the reason why some who are dear to God have this kind of punishment never forgiven, but it abides with them to their lives' end, goes with them to the day of their death, yea, is the very cause of their death. By this punishment they are cut off out of the land of the living. But all this is that they might 'not be condemned with the world.'[3]

Christ died not to save from this punishment; Christ intercedes not to save from this punishment. Nothing but a good life will save from this punishment; nor always that either.

The hidings of God's face, the harshness of his providences, the severe and sharp chastisements that ofttimes overtake the very spirits

1 Matthew 6:14–15.
2 Matthew 6:15; 18:28–35.
3 1 Corinthians 11:32.

of his people, plainly show that Christ died not to save from temporal punishments, prays not to save from temporal punishments—that is, absolutely. God has reserved a power to punish, with temporal punishments, the best and dearest of his people, if need be.[1] And sometimes he remits them, sometimes not, even as it pleases him. I come now to the second thing.

CHRIST SAVES TO THE UTTERMOST

Second, I shall now show you something of what it is for Christ, by his intercession, to save to the '*uttermost*.' 'He is able to save them to the uttermost.'

This is a great expression, and carrieth with it much. 'Uttermost' signifieth to the outside, to the end, to the last, to the furthest part. And it hath respect both to persons and things.[2]

1. To persons. Some persons are in their own apprehensions even further from Christ than anybody else; afar off, a great way off, yet a-coming, as the prodigal was. Now, these many times are exceedingly afraid; the sight of that distance that they think is betwixt Christ and them makes them afraid. As it is said in another case, 'They that dwell in the uttermost parts are afraid at thy tokens.'[3] So these are afraid they shall not speed, not obtain that for which they come to God. But the text says, He is able to save to the uttermost, to the very hindermost, them that come to God by him.

Two sorts of men seem to be far, very far from God. (1.) The town sinner. (2.) The great backslider.[4] But both these, if they come, he is able to save to the uttermost. He is able to save them from all those dangers that they fear will prevent their obtaining of that grace

---

1 One proof of a future state of rewards is, that many of God's dearest saints have been most bitterly persecuted all their lives, and martyred with extreme cruelty. Thus it was with the greatest man this country ever saw—William Tyndale, to whom the world is indebted for our translation of the Bible. See his letters, in his Memoir by Offor, prefixed to a reprint of the first English New Testament.—OFFOR.

2 Genesis 49:26; Deuteronomy 30:4; Matthew 5:26; Mark 13:27; Luke 15.

3 Psalm 65:8.

4 Nehemiah 1:9.

and mercy they would have to help them in time of need. The publicans and harlots enter into the kingdom of heaven.

2. As this text respecteth persons, so it respecteth things. There are some things with which some are attended that are coming to God, by Christ, that make their coming hard and very difficult.

(1.) There is a more than ordinary breaking up of the corruptions of their nature. It seems as if all their lusts and vile passions of the flesh were become masters, and migth now do what they will with the soul. Yea, they take this man and toss and tumble him like a ball in a large place. This man is not master of himself, of his thoughts, nor of his passions—'His iniquities, like the wind, do carry him away.'[1] He thinks to go forward, but this wind blows him backward; he laboureth against this wind, but cannot find that he getteth ground; he takes what advantage opportunity doth minister to him, but all he gets is to be beat out of heart, out of breath, out of courage. He stands still, and pants, and gapeth as for life. 'I opened my mouth, and panted,' said David, 'for I longed for thy commandments.'[2] He sets forward again, but has nothing but labour and sorrow.

(2.) Nay, to help forward his calamity, Satan [and his] angels will not be wanting, both to trouble his head with the fumes of their stinking breath, nor to throw up his heels in their dirty places—'And as he was yet a-coming, the devil threw him down and tare *him*.'[3] How many strange, hideous, and amazing blasphemies have those, some of those, that are coming to Christ, had injected and fixed upon their spirits against him. Nothing so common to such, as to have some hellish wish or other against God they are coming to, and against Christ, by whom they would come to him. These blasphemies are like those frogs that I have heard of, that will leap up, and catch hold of, and hang by their claws. Now help, Lord; now, Lord Jesus, what shall I do? Now, Son of David, have mercy upon me! I say, to say these words is hard work for such an one. But he is able to

---

1 Isaiah 64:6.
2 Psalm 119:131.
3 Luke 9:42.

save to the uttermost this comer to God by him.

(3.) There are also the oppositions of sense and reason hard at work for the devil, against the soul; the men of his own house are risen up against him. One's sense and reason, one would think, should not fall in with the devil against ourselves, and yet nothing more common, nothing more natural, than for our own sense and reason to turn the unnatural, and war both against our God and us. And now it is hard coming to God. Better can a man hear and deal with any objections against himself, than with those that himself doth make against himself. They lie close, stick fast, speak aloud, and will be heard; yea, will haunt and hunt him, as the devil doth some, in every hole and corner. But come, man, come; for he is able to save to the uttermost!

(4.) Now guilt is the consequence and fruit of all this; and what so intolerable a burden as guilt! They talk of the stones, and of the sands of the sea; but it is guilt that breaks the heart with its burden. And Satan has the art of making the uttermost of every sin; he can blow it up, make it swell, make every hair of its head as big as a cedar. He can tell how to make it a heinous offence, an unpardonable offence, an offence of that continuance, and committed against so much light, that, says he, it is impossible it should ever be forgiven. But, soul, Christ is able to save to the uttermost, he can 'do exceeding abundantly above all that we ask or think.'[1]

(5.) Join to all this the rage and terror of men, which thing of itself is sufficient to quash and break to pieces all desires to come to God by Christ; yea, and it doth do so to thousands that are not willing to go to hell. Yet thou art kept, and made to go panting on; a whole world of men, and devils, and sin, are not able to keep thee from coming. But how comes it to pass that thou art so hearty, that thou settest thy face against so much wind and weather? I dare say it arises not from thyself, nor from any of thine enemies. This comes from God, though thou art not aware thereof; and is obtained for thee by the intercession of the blessed Son of God, who is also able to save thee to the uttermost, that comest to God by him.

1 Ephesians 3:20.

(6.) And for a conclusion as to this, I will add, that there is much of the honour of the Lord Jesus engaged as to the saving of the *coming* man to the uttermost: 'I am glorified in them,' saith he.[1] He is exalted to be a Saviour.[2] And if the blessed One doth count it an exaltation to be a Saviour, surely it is an exaltation to be a Saviour, and a great one. 'They shall cry unto the Lord because of the oppressors, and he shall send them a Saviour, and a great one, and he shall deliver them.'[3] If it is a glory to be a Saviour, a great Saviour, then it is a glory for a Saviour, a great one, to save, and save, and save to the uttermost—to the uttermost man, to the uttermost sin, to the uttermost temptation. And hence it is that he saith again, speaking of the transgressions, sins, and iniquities that he would pardon, that it should turn to him for 'a name of joy, a praise, and an honour before all nations.'[4] He therefore counts it an honour to be a great Saviour, to save men to the uttermost.

When Moses said, 'I beseech thee, show me thy glory,' the answer was, 'I will make all my goodness pass before thee, and I will proclaim the name of the Lord before thee.'[5] And when he came indeed to make proclamation, then he proclaimed, 'The LORD, The LORD God, merciful and gracious, long-suffering, and abundant in goodness and truth, keeping mercy for thousands, forgiving iniquity and transgression and sin, and that will by no means clear *the guilty*.'[6] That will by no means clear them that will not come to me that they may be saved.

See here, if it is not by himself accounted his glory to make his goodness, all his goodness, pass before us. And how can that be, if he saveth not to the uttermost them that come unto God by him? For goodness is by us noways seen but by those acts by which it expresseth itself to be so. And, I am sure, to save, to save to the uttermost, is one of the most eminent expressions by which we understand it is great

---

1 John 17:10.
2 Acts 5:31.
3 Isaiah 19:20.
4 Jeremiah 33:9.
5 Exodus 33:18–19.
6 Exodus 34:6–7.

goodness. I know goodness has many ways to express itself to be what it is to the world; but then it expresseth its greatness when it pardons and saves, when it pardons and saves to the uttermost. My goodness, says Christ, extends not itself to my Father, but to my saints.[1] My Father has no need of my goodness, but my saints have, and therefore it shall reach forth itself for their help, in whom is all my delight. And, 'Oh how great *is* thy goodness, which thou hast laid up for them that fear thee; *which* thou hast wrought for them that trust in thee before the sons of men!'[2] It is therefore that which tendeth to get Christ a name, a fame, and glory, to be able to save to the uttermost them that come to God by him.

In Christ's ability to save, lieth our safety

But some may say, What is the meaning of this word *able?* 'Wherefore he is *able* to save.' He is able to save to the uttermost. How comes it to pass that his power to save is rather put in than his willingness; for willingness, saith the soul, would better have pleased me. I will speak two or three words to this question. And,

First, By this word *able* is suggested to us the sufficiency of his merit, the great worthiness of his merit; for, as Intercessor, he sticks fast by his merit; all his petitions, prayers, or supplications are grounded upon the worthiness of his person as Mediator, and on the validity of his offering as priest. This is the more clear, if you consider the reason why those priests and sacrifices under the law could not make the worshippers perfect. It was, I say, because there wanted in them worthiness and merit in their sacrifices. But this man, when he came and offered his sacrifice, he did by that one act 'perfect for ever them that are sanctified,' or set apart for glory. 'But this *man*, after he had offered one sacrifice for sins, for ever sat down on the right hand of God.'[3]

1 Psalm 16:2–3.
2 Psalm 31:19.
3 Hebrews 10:1–12.

When Moses prayed for the people of Israel, thus he said, 'And now, I beseech thee, let the power of my Lord be great, according as thou hast spoken.' But what had he spoken? 'The LORD is long-suffering, and of great mercy, forgiving iniquity and transgression, and by no means clearing *the guilty* . . . Pardon, I beseech thee, the iniquity of this people according unto the greatness of thy mercy, and as thou hast forgiven this people, from Egypt even until now.'[1]

Second, Has he but power, we know he is willing, else he would not have promised; it is also his glory to pardon and save. So, then, in his *ability* lies our safety. What if he were never so willing, if he were not of ability sufficient, what would his willingness do? But he has showed, as I said, his willingness by promising: 'Him that cometh to me I will in no wise cast out.'[2] So that now our comfort lies in his power, in that he is able to make good his word.[3] And this also will then be seen, when he hath saved them that come to God by him, when he hath saved them to the uttermost; not to the uttermost of his ability, but to the uttermost of our necessity; for to the uttermost of his ability I believe he will never be put to it to save his church; not for that he is loath *so* to save, but because there is no need so to save; he shall not need to put out all his power, and to press the utmost of his merit for the saving of his church. Alas! there is sufficiency of merit in him to save a thousand times as many more as are like to be saved by him; 'he is able to do exceeding abundantly above all that we ask or think.' Measure not, therefore, what he can do by what he has, doth, or will do; neither do thou interpret this word, to the *uttermost*, as if it related to the uttermost of his ability, but rather as it relateth, for so it doth indeed, to the greatness of thy necessity. For as he is able to save thee, though thy condition be, as it may be supposed to be, the worst that ever man was in that was saved, so he is able to save thee, though thy condition were ten times worse than it is.

What! shall not the worthiness of the Son of God be sufficient to

---

1 Numbers 14:17–19.
2 John 6:37.
3 Romans 4:20–21.

save from the sin of man? or shall the sin of the world be of that weight
to destroy, that it shall put Christ Jesus to the uttermost of the worth
of his person and merit to save therefrom? I believe it is blasphemy to
think so. We can easily imagine that he can save all the world—that
is, that he is of ability to do it; but we cannot imagine that he can do
no more than we can think he can. But our imagination and thoughts
set no bound to his ability. 'He is able to do exceeding abundantly
above all that we ask or think.' But what that is, I say, no man can
think, no man can imagine. So, then, Jesus Christ can do more than
ever any man thought he could do as to saving; he can do we know
not what. This, therefore, should encourage comers to come to him;
and them that come, to hope. This, I say, should encourage them to
let out, to lengthen, and heighten their thoughts by the word, to the
uttermost, seeing he can 'save to the uttermost them that come to
God by him.'[1]

INFERENCES FROM THE BENEFITS OF CHRIST'S INTERCESSION

Third. And now I come to the third thing that I told you I should
speak to, and that is, to *those inferences that may be gathered from
these words.*

1. Are they that are justified by Christ's blood such as have need
yet to be saved by his intercession? *Then from hence it follows that
justification will stand with imperfection.* It doth not therefore follow that a justified man is without infirmity; for he that is without
infirmity—that is, perfect with absolute perfection, has no need to
be yet saved by an act yet to be performed by a mediator and his
mediation.

When I say, justification will stand with imperfection, I do not
mean that it will allow, countenance, or approve thereof; but I mean

---

1 'The uttermost.' How boundless! It includes all that wondrous extent of Divine love
which we shall be ever learning, and never be able to comprehend, the breadth, length,
depth, and height of the love of Christ, which passeth knowledge.—OFFOR.

there is no necessity of our perfection, of our personal perfection, as to our justification, and that we are justified without it; yea, that that, in justified persons, remains. Again; when I say that justification will stand with imperfection, I do not mean that in our justification we are imperfect; for in that we are complete; 'we are complete in him' who is our justice.[1] If otherwise, the imperfection is in the matter that justifieth us, which is the righteousness of Christ. Yea, and to say so would conclude that wrong judgment proceedeth from him that imputeth that righteousness to us to justification, since an imperfect thing is imputed to us for justification. But far be it from any that believe that God is true to imagine such a thing; all his works are perfect, there is nothing wanting in them as to the present design.

Question. But what then do we mean when we say, justification will stand with a state of imperfection?

Answer. Why, I mean that justified men are yet sinners in themselves, are yet full of imperfections; yea, sinful imperfections. Justified Paul said, 'I know that in me, that is, in my flesh, dwelleth no good thing.'[2] While we are yet sinners, we are justified by the blood of Christ. Hence, again, it is said, 'he justifieth the ungodly.'[3] Justification, then, only covereth our sin from the sight of God; it maketh us not perfect with inherent perfection. But God, for the sake of that righteousness which by his grace is imputed to us, declareth us quit and discharged from the curse, and sees sin in us no more to condemnation.

Why the justified need an intercessor

And this is the reason, or one reason, why they that are justified have need of an intercessor—to wit, to save us from the evil of the sin that remains in our flesh after we are justified by grace through Christ, and set free from the law as to condemnation. Therefore, as it is said,

---

1 Colossians 2:10.
2 Romans 7:18.
3 Romans 4:5; 5:8–9.

we are saved; so it is said, 'He is able also to save them to the uttermost that come unto God by him, seeing he ever liveth to make intercession for them.' The godly, for now we will call them the godly, though there is yet abundance of sin in them, feel in themselves many things even after justification by which they are convinced they are still attended with personal, sinful imperfections.

Imperfect in their feelings and inclinations.

(1.) They feel unbelief, fear, mistrust, doubting, despondings, murmurings, blasphemies, pride, lightness, foolishness, avarice, fleshly lusts, heartlessness to good, wicked desires, low thoughts of Christ, too good thoughts of sin, and, at times, too great an itching after the worst of immoralities.

(2.) They feel in themselves an aptness to incline to errors, as to lean to the works of the law for justification; to question the truth of the resurrection and judgment to come; to dissemble and play the hypocrite in profession and in performance of duties; to do religious duties rather to please man than God, who trieth the heart.

(3.) They feel an inclination in them, in times of trial, to faint under the cross, to seek too much to save themselves, to dissemble the known truth for the obtaining a little favour with men, and to speak things that they ought not, that they may sleep in a whole skin.

(4.) They feel wearisomeness in religious duties, but a natural propensity to things of the flesh. They feel a desire to go beyond bounds both at board, and bed, and bodily exercise, and in all lawful recreation.

(5.) They feel in themselves an aptness to take the advantage of using of things that are lawful, as food, raiment, sleep, talk, estates, relations, beauty, wit, parts, and graces, to unlawful ends. These things, with many more of the like kind, the justified man finds and feels in himself, to his humbling and often casting down; and to save him from the destroying evil of these, Christ ever liveth to make intercession for him.

Imperfect in their graces.—Again; the justified man is imperfect in his graces, and therefore needeth to be saved by the intercession of Christ from the bad fruit that that imperfection yields.

Justifying righteousness is accompanied with graces—the graces of the Spirit. Though these graces are not that matter by and through which we are justified, nor any part thereof, that being only the obedience of Christ imputed to us of mere pleasure and good will; but, I say, they come when justification comes.[1] And though they are not so easily discerned at the first, they show forth themselves afterwards. But I say, how many soever they are, and how fast soever they grow, their utmost arrivement here is but a state short of perfection. None of the graces of God's Spirit in our hearts can do their work in us without shortness, and that because of their own imperfections, and also because of the oppositions that they meet with from our flesh.

(1.) Faith, which is the root-grace, the grand grace, its shortness is sufficiently manifest by its shortness of apprehension of things pertaining to the person, offices, relations, and works of Christ, now in the heavenly place for us. It is also very defective in its fetching of comfort from the Word to us, and in continuing of it with us, when at any time we attain unto it; in its receiving of strength to subdue sin, and in its purifyings of the heart, though indeed it doth what it doth in reality, yet how short is it of doing of it thoroughly? Oftentimes, were it not for supplies by virtue of the intercession of Christ, faith would fail of performing its office in any measure.[2]

(2.) There is hope, another grace of the Spirit bestowed upon us; and how often is that also, as to the excellency of working, made to flag? 'I shall perish,' saith David; 'I am cut off from before thine eyes,' said he.[3] And now where was his hope, in the right gospel discovery of it? Also all our fear of men, and fears of death, and fears of judgment, they arise from the imperfections of hope. But from all those faults Christ saves us by his intercessions.

(3.) There is love, that should be in us as hot as fire. It is compared to fire, to fire of the hottest sort; yea, it is said to be hotter than the coals of juniper.[4] But who finds this heat in love so much as for

1 Romans 9.
2 Luke 22:31–32.
3 Psalm 31:22.
4 Song of Solomon 8:6–7.

one poor quarter of an hour together? Some little flashes, perhaps, some at some times may feel, but where is that constant burning of affection that the Word, the love of God, and the love of Christ call for? yea, and that the necessities of the poor and afflicted members of Christ call for also. Ah! love is cold in these frozen days, and short when it is at the highest.

(4.) The grace of humility, when is it? who has a thimbleful thereof? Where is he that is 'clothed with humility,' and that does what he is commanded 'with all humility of mind?'[1]

(5.) For zeal, where is that also? Zeal for God against sin, profaneness, superstition, and idolatry. I speak now to the godly, who have this zeal in the root and habit; but oh, how little of it puts forth itself into actions in such a day as this is!

(6.) There is reverence, fear, and standing in awe of God's Word and judgments, where are the excellent workings thereof to be found? And where it is most, how far short of perfect acts is it?

(7.) Simplicity and godly sincerity also, with how much dirt is it mixed in the best; especially among those of the saints that are rich, who have got the poor and beggarly art of complimenting? For the more compliment, the less sincerity. Many words will not fill a bushel. But 'in the multitude of words there wanteth not sin.'[2] Plain men are thin come up in this day; to find a mouth without fraud and deceit now is a rare thing. Thus might one count up all the graces of the Spirit, and show wherein every one of them are scanty and wanting of perfection. Now look, what they want of perfection is supplied with sin and vanity; for there is a fulness of sin and flesh at hand to make up all the vacant places in our souls. There is no place in the souls of the godly but it is filled up with darkness when the light is wanting, and with sin so far forth as grace is wanting. Satan, also, diligently waiteth to come in at the door, if Careless has left it a little achare.[3]

---

1 1 Peter 5:5; Acts 20:19.

2 Proverbs 10:19.

3 Achare—from to chare, to turn about, or backwards and forwards; as, achare woman, one who takes her turn at work; a door achare, or ajar, turning to and fro on its hinges, or standing partly open.—OFFOR.

But, oh! the grace of our Lord Jesus Christ, who ever liveth to make intercession for us, and that, by so doing, saves us from all the imperfect acts and workings of our graces, and from all the advantages that flesh, and sin, and Satan getteth upon us thereby.

Imperfect in their Duties.—Further, as Christ Jesus our Lord doth save us, by his intercession, from that hurt that would unavoidably come upon us by these, so also, by that we are saved from the evil that is at any time found in any or all our holy duties and performances that is our duty daily to be found in. That our duties are imperfect, follows upon what was discoursed before; for if our graces be imperfect, how can our duties but be so too?

(1.) Our prayers, how imperfect are they! With how much unbelief are they mixed! How apt is our tongue to run, in prayer, before our hearts! With how much earnestness do our lips move, while our hearts lie within as cold as a clod! Yea, and ofttimes, it is to be feared, we ask for that with our mouth that we care not whether we have or no. Where is the man that pursues with all his might what but now he seemed to ask for with all his heart? Prayer is become a shell, a piece of formality, a very empty thing, as to the spirit and life of prayer at this day. I speak now of the prayers of the godly. I once met with a poor woman that, in the greatest of her distresses, told me she did use to rise in the night, in cold weather, and pray to God, while she sweat with fears of the loss of her prayer and desires that her soul might be saved. I have heard of many that have *played*, but of few that have *prayed*, till they have sweat, by reason of their wrestling with God for mercy in that duty.

(2.) There is the duty of almsgiving, another gospel performance; but how poorly is it done in our days! We have so many foolish ways to lay out money, in toys and fools' baubles for our children, that we can spare none, or very little, for the relief of the poor. Also, do not many give that to their dogs, yea, let it lie in their houses until it stinks so vilely that neither dog nor cat will eat it; which, had it been bestowed well in time, might have been a succour and nourishment to some poor member of Christ?

(3.) There is hearing of the Word; but, alas! the place of hearing is the place of sleeping with many a fine professor. I have often observed that those that keep shops can briskly attend upon a two-penny customer; but when they come themselves to God's market, they spend their time too much in letting their thoughts to wander from God's commandments, or in a nasty drowsy way. The heads, also, and hearts of most hearers are to the Word as the sieve is to water; they can hold no sermons, remember no texts, bring home no proofs, produce none of the sermon to the edification and profit of others. And do not the best take up too much in hearing, and mind too little what, by the Word, God calls for at their hands, to perform it with a good conscience?

(4.) There is faithfulness in callings, faithfulness to brethren, faithfulness to the world, faithfulness to children, to servants, to all, according to our place and capacity. Oh! how little of it is there found in the mouths and lives, to speak nothing of the hearts, of professors.

I will proceed no further in this kind of repetition of things; only thus much give me leave to say over again, even many of the truly godly are very faulty here. But what would they do if there were not one always at the right hand of God, by intercession, taking away these kind of iniquities?

2. Are those that are justified by the blood of Christ such, after that, as have need also of saving by Christ's intercession? From hence, then, we may infer, that as sin, so *Satan will not give over from assaulting the best of the saints.*

It is not justification that can secure us from being assaulted by Satan: 'Simon, Simon, Satan has desired to have you.'[1] There are two things that do encourage the devil to set upon the people of God:—

(1.) He knows not who are elect; for all that profess are not, and, therefore, he will make trial, if he can get them into his sieve, whether he can cause them to perish. And great success he hath had this way. Many a brave professor has he overcome; he has cast some of the stars from heaven to earth; he picked one out from among the apostles,

---

1 Luke 22:31–32.

and one, as it is thought, from among the seven deacons,[1] and many from among Christ's disciples; but how many, think you, nowadays, doth he utterly destroy with his net?

(2.) If it so happeneth that he cannot destroy, because Christ, by his intercession, prevaileth, yet will he set upon the church to defile and afflict it. For (*a.*), If he can but get us to fall, with Peter, then he has obtained that dishonour be brought to God, the weak to be stumbled, the world offended, and the gospel vilified and reproached. Or (*b.*), If he cannot throw up our heels, yet, by buffeting of us, he can grieve us, afflict us, put us to pain, fright us, drive us to many doubts, and make our life very uncomfortable unto us, and make us go groaning to our Father's house. But blessed be God for his Christ, and for that 'he ever liveth to make intercession for us.'

3. Are those that are justified by the blood of Christ such as, after that, have need to be saved by Christ's intercession? Then, hence I infer that *it is dangerous going about anything in our own name and strength*. If we would have helps from the intercession of Christ, let us have a care that we do what we do according to the word of Christ. Do what he bids us as well as we can, as he bids us, and then we need not doubt to have help and salvation in those duties by the intercession of Christ. '*Do* all,' says the apostle, 'in the name of the Lord Jesus.'[2] Oh, but then the devil and the world will be most of all offended! Well, well, but if you do nothing but as in his fear, by his Word, in his name, you may be sure of what help his intercession can afford you, and that can afford you much help, not only to begin, but to go through with your work in some good measure, as you should; and by that also you shall be secured from those dangers, if not temptations to dangers, that those that go out about business in their own names and strength shall be sure to meet withal.

4. Are those that are justified by the blood of Christ such as, after that, have need of being saved by Christ's intercession? Then, hence I

---

1 It is supposed by some that 'Nicolas' was the founder of the sect of the Nicolaitanes, mentioned in Revelation 2:6, 15; but of this there is much doubt. See Dr. Gill, and Matthew Henry on Acts 6:5.—OFFOR.

2 Colossians 3:17.

infer again, *that God has a great dislike of the sins of his own people, and would fall upon them in judgment and anger much more severely than he doth, were it not for Christ's intercession.* The gospel is not, as some think, a loose and licentious doctrine, nor God's discipline of his church a negligent and careless discipline; for, though those that believe already have also an intercessor, yet God, to show detestation against sin, doth often make them feel to purpose the weight of his fingers. The sincere, that fain would walk oft with God, have felt what I say, and that to the breaking of their bones full oft. The loose ones, and those that God loves not, may be utter strangers as to this; but those that are his own indeed do know it is otherwise.[1] 'You only have I known' above all others, says God, 'therefore I will punish you for all your iniquities.'[2] God keeps a very strict house among his children. David found it so, Haman found it so, Job found it so, and the church of God found it so; and I know not that his mind is ever the less against sin, notwithstanding we have an Intercessor. True, our Intercessor saves us from damning evils, from damning judgments; but he neither doth nor will secure us from temporal punishment, from spiritual punishment, unless we watch, deny ourselves, and walk in his fear. I would to God that those who are otherwise minded did but feel, for three or four months, something of what I have felt for several years together for base sinful *thoughts!* I wish it, I say, if it might be for their good, and for the better regulating of their understandings. But whether they obtain my wish or no, sure I am that God is no countenancer of sin; no, not in his own people; nay, he will bear it least of all in them. And as for others, however he may for a while have patience towards them, if, perhaps, his goodness may lead them to repentance; yet the day is coming when he will pay the carnal and hypocrites' home with devouring fire for their offences.

But if our holy God will not let us go altogether unpunished, though we have so able and blessed an Intercessor, that has always to

---

1 A godly man's prayers are sometimes answered by terrible things in righteousness. He prays to be quickened in his walk with God; and the answer, dictated by wisdom and love, is the loss of some temporal blessing, that he may be kept 'looking unto Jesus.'—OFFOR.
2 Amos 3:2.

present God with, on our behalf, so valuable a price of his own blood, now before the throne of grace, what should we have done if there had been no day's-man, none to plead for us, or to make intercession on our behalf? Read that text, 'For I *am* with thee, saith the LORD, to save thee; though I make a full end of all nations whither I have scattered thee, yet will I not make a full end of thee; but I will correct thee in measure, and will not leave thee altogether unpunished.'[1] If it be so, I say, what had become of us, if we had had no Intercessor? And what will become of them concerning whom the Lord has said already, 'I will not take up their names into my lips?'[2] 'I pray not for the world.'[3]

5. Are those that are already justified by the blood of Christ yet such as have need of being saved by his intercession? Then, hence, I infer that *Christ is not only the beginner, but the completer of our salvation;* or, as the Holy Ghost calls him, 'the author and finisher of *our* faith,'[4] or, as it calls him again, 'the author of eternal salvation.'[5] Of salvation throughout, from the beginning to the end, from first to last. His hands have laid the foundation of it in his own blood, and his hands shall finish it by his intercession.[6] As he has laid the beginning fastly, so he shall bring forth the headstones with shoutings, and we shall cry, Grace, grace, at the last, salvation only belongeth to the Lord.[7]

Many there be that begin with grace, and end with works, and think THAT is the only way. Indeed works will save from temporal punishments, when their imperfections are purged from them by the intercession of Christ; but to be saved and brought to glory, to be carried through this dangerous world, from my first moving after Christ till I set my foot within the gates of paradise, this is the work of my Mediator, of my high priest and intercessor; it is he that fetches

1 Jeremiah 30:11.
2 Psalm 16:4.
3 John 17:9.
4 Hebrews 12:2.
5 Hebrews 5:9.
6 Zechariah 4:9.
7 Zechariah 4:7; Psalm 3:8; Isaiah 43:11.

us again when we are run away; it is he that lifteth us up when the devil and sin has thrown us down; it is he that quickeneth us when we grow cold; it is he that comforteth us when we despair; it is he that obtains fresh pardon when we have contracted sin; and he that purges our consciences when they are loaden with guilt.[1]

I know also, that rewards do wait for them in heaven that do believe in Christ, and shall do well on earth; but this is not a reward of merit, but of grace. We are saved by Christ; brought to glory by Christ; and all our works are no otherwise made acceptable to God but by the person and personal excellencies and works of Christ; therefore, whatever the jewels are, and the bracelets, and the pearls, that thou shalt be adorned with as a reward of service done to God in the world, for them thou must thank Christ, and, before all, confess that he was the meritorious cause thereof.[2] He saves us, and saves our services too.[3] They would be all cast back as dung in our faces, were they not rinsed and washed in the blood, were they not sweetened and perfumed in the incense, and conveyed to God himself through the white hand of Jesus Christ; for that is his golden censer; from thence ascends the smoke that is in the nostrils of God of such a sweet savour.[4]

6. Are those that are already justified by the blood of Christ, such as do still stand in need of being saved by his intercession? Then hence I infer again, that *we that have been saved hitherto, and preserved from the dangers that we have met with since our first conversion to this moment, should ascribe the glory to Jesus Christ, to God by Jesus Christ.* 'I have prayed that thy faith fail not: I pray that thou wouldest keep them from the evil,' is the true cause of our standing, and of our continuing in the faith and holy profession of the gospel to this very day. Wherefore we must give the glory of all to God by Christ: 'I will not trust in my bow,' said David, 'neither shall my sword save me. But thou hast saved us from our enemies, and hast

1 Ezekiel 34:16; Psalm 145:14.
2 1 Peter 2:5; Hebrews 13:15.
3 Revelation 5:9–14.
4 Revelation 7:12–14; 8:3–4.

put them to shame that hated us. In God we boast all the day long, and praise thy name for ever. Selah!' 'He always causeth us to triumph in Christ.' 'We rejoice in Christ Jesus, and have no confidence in the flesh.'[1] Thus you see that, both in the Old and New Testament, all the glory is given to the Lord, as well for preservation to heaven as for justification of life. And he that is well acquainted with himself will do this readily; though light heads, and such as are not acquainted with the desperate evil that is in their natures, will sacrifice to their own net. But such will so sacrifice but a while. Sir Death is coming, and he will put them into the view of what they see not now, and will feed sweetly upon them, because they made not the Lord their trust. And therefore, ascribe thou the glory of the preservation of thy soul in the faith hitherto, to that salvation which Christ Jesus our Lord obtaineth for thee by his intercession.

7. Are those that are already justified by the blood of Christ such as do still stand in need of being saved by his intercession? Then is this also to be inferred from hence, *that saints should look to him for that saving that they shall yet have need of betwixt this and the day of their dissolution;* yea, from henceforward, even to the day of judgment. I say, they should still look to him for the remaining part of their salvation, or for that of their salvation which is yet behind; and let them look for it with confidence, for that it is in a faithful hand; and for thy encouragement to look and hope for the completing of thy salvation in glory, let me present thee with a few things—

(1.) The hardest or worst part of the work of thy Saviour is over; his bloody work, his bearing of thy sin and curse, his loss of the light of his Father's face for a time; his dying upon the cursed tree, that was the worst, the sorest, the hardest, and most difficult part of the work of redemption; and yet this he did willingly, cheerfully, and without thy desires; yea, this he did, as considering those for whom he did it in a state of rebellion and enmity to him.

(2.) Consider, also, that he has made a beginning with thy soul to reconcile thee to God, and to that end has bestowed his justice upon

1 Psalm 44:6–8; 2 Corinthians 2:14; Philippians 3:3.

thee, put his Spirit within thee, and began to make the unweldable mountain and rock,[1] thy heart, to turn towards him, and desire after him; to believe in him, and rejoice in him.

(3.) Consider, also, that some comfortable pledges of his love thou hast already received, namely, as to feel the sweetness of his love, as to see the light of his countenance, as to be made to know his power in raising of thee when thou wast down, and how he has made thee stand, while hell has been pushing at thee, utterly to overthrow thee.

(4.) Thou mayest consider, also, that what remains behind of the work of thy salvation in his hands, as it is the most easy part, so the most comfortable, and that part which will more immediately issue in his glory, and therefore he will mind it.

(5.) That which is behind is also more safe in his hand than if it were in thine own; he is wise, he is powerful, he is faithful, and therefore will manage that part that is lacking to our salvation well, until he has completed it. It is his love to thee that has made him that 'he putteth no trust in thee;' he knows that he can himself bring thee to his kingdom most surely; and therefore has not left that work to thee, no, not any part thereof.[2]

Live in hope, then, in a lively hope, that since Christ is risen from the dead, he lives to make intercession for thee, and that thou shalt reap the blessed benefit of this twofold salvation that is wrought, and that is working out for thee, by Jesus Christ our Lord. And thus have we treated of the benefit of his intercession, in that he is able to save to the uttermost. And this leads me to the third particular.

---

1 The heart 'unweldable.' This homely allusion, drawn from Bunyan's trade of blacksmith, is worthy of remark. The heart a mountain of iron, so hard that no heat in nature can soften it so as to weld it to Christ. *To weld* is to hammer into firm union two pieces of iron, when heated almost to fusion, so as to become *one piece*. The heart of man is by nature 'unweldable,' until God the Spirit softens it; and then the *union* is such that Christ becomes THE LIFE of his saints. Reader, has thy heart passed through this process?—OFFOR.
2 Job 5:18; 15:15.

CHAPTER III

THE PERSONS INTERESTED IN THE INTERCESSION OF CHRIST

THIRD, The third particular is to show WHO ARE THE PERSONS INTERESTED IN THIS INTERCESSION OF CHRIST; and they are *those that come to God by him.* The words are very concise, and distinctly laid down; they are they that come, that come to God, that come to God by him. 'Wherefore he is able also to save them, to save to the uttermost them that come to God by him, seeing he ever liveth to make intercession for them.'

Of coming to God by Christ.—A little, first, to comment upon the order of the words, 'that come unto God by him.'

There are that come unto God, *but not 'by him;'* and these are not included in this text, have not a share in this privilege. Thus the Jews came to God, the unbelieving Jews, 'who had a zeal of God, but not according to knowledge.'[1] These submitted not to Christ, the righteousness of God, but thought to come to him by works of their own, or at least, as it were, by them, and so came short of salvation by grace, for that reigns to salvation only in Christ. To these Christ's person and undertakings were a stumbling stone: for at him they stumbled, and did split themselves to pieces, though they indeed were such as came to God for life.

COME TO CHRIST, BUT NOT TO GOD BY HIM

As there are that come to God, but not by Christ, *so there are that*

1 Romans 9:30–34; 10:1–4.

come to Christ, but not to God by him:[1] of this sort are they, who hearing that Christ is Saviour, therefore come to him for pardon, but cannot abide to come to God by him, for that he is holy, and so will snub their lusts, and will change their hearts and natures. Mind me what I say. There are a great many that would be saved by Christ, but love not to be sanctified by God through him. These make a stop at Christ, and will go no further. Might such have pardon, they care not whether ever they went to heaven or no. Of this kind of coming to Christ I think it is, of which he warneth his disciples when he saith, 'In that day ye shall ask me nothing. Verily, verily, I say unto you, Whatsoever ye shall ask the Father in my name, he will give *it* you.'[2] As who should say, when you ask for anything, make not a stop at me, but come to my Father by me; for they that come to me, and not to my Father, through me, will have nothing of what they come for. Righteousness shall be imputed to us, 'if we believe on him that raised up Jesus our Lord from the dead.'[3] To come to Christ for a benefit, and stop there, and not come to God by him, prevaileth nothing. Here the mother of Zebedee's children erred; and about this it was that the Lord Jesus cautioned her. Lord, saith she, 'Grant that these my two sons may sit, the one on thy right hand, and the other on the left, in thy kingdom.' But what is the answer of Christ? 'To sit on my right hand and on my left, is not mine to give, but for whom it is prepared of my Father.'[4] As who should say, Woman, of myself I do nothing, my Father worketh with me. Go therefore to him by me, for I am the way to him; what thou canst obtain of him by me thou shalt have; that is to say, what of the things that pertain to eternal life, whether pardon or glory.

It is true, the Son has power to give pardon and glory, but he

---

1 This is a solemn and heart searching consideration. It is not enough that we fear eternal wrath, but we must love heaven, for the sake of its purity. It is not sufficient that we go to Christ for pardon, but we must go through him to the infinitely holy God, for holiness and fitness for heaven.—OFFOR.

2 John 16:23.

3 Romans 4:24–25.

4 Matthew 20:21–23.

gives it not by himself, but by and according to the will of his Father.[1] They, therefore, that come to him for an eternal good, and look not to the Father by him, come short thereof; I mean, now, pardon and glory. And hence, though it be said the Son of man hath power on earth to forgive sins—to wit, to show the certainty of his Godhead, and of the excellency of his mediation; yet forgiveness of sin is said to lie more particularly in the hand of the Father, and that God for Christ's sake forgiveth us.[2]

The Father, as we see, will not forgive unless we come to him by the Son. Why, then, should we conceit that the Son will forgive those that come not to the Father by him?

So then, justifying righteousness is in the Son, and with him also is intercession; but forgiveness is with the Father; yea, the gift of the Holy Ghost, yea, and the power of imputing of the righteousness of Christ is yet in the hand of the Father. Hence Christ prays to the Father to forgive, prays to the Father to send the Spirit, and it is God that imputeth righteousness to justification to us.[3] The Father, then, doth nothing but for the sake of and through the Son; the Son also doth nothing derogating from the glory of the Father. But it would be a derogation to the glory of the Father if the Son should grant to save them that come not to the Father by him; wherefore you that cry Christ, Christ, delighting yourselves in the thoughts of forgiveness, but care not to come by Christ to the Father for it, you are not at all concerned in this blessed text, for he only saves by his intercession them that come to God by him.

There are three sorts of people that may be said to come to Christ, but not to God by him.

1. They whose utmost design in coming is only that guilt and fear of damning may be removed from them. And there are three signs of such an one—(1.) He that takes up in a belief of pardon, and so goes on in his course of carnality as he did before. (2.) He whose

---

1 Matthew 9:6; John 17:22.
2 Ephesians 4:32.
3 Luke 23:34; John 14:16; Romans 4:6.

comfort in the belief of pardon standeth alone, without other fruits of the Holy Ghost. (3.) He that, having been washed, can be content to tumble in the mire, as the sow again, or as the dog that did spue to lick up his vomit again.

2. They may be said to come to Christ, but not to God by him, who do pick and choose doctrines, itching only after that which sounds of grace,[1] but secretly abhorring of that which presseth to moral goodness. These did never see God, what notions soever they may have of the Lord Jesus, and of forgiveness from him.[2]

3. They surely did never come to God by Christ, however they may boast of the grace of Christ, that will from the freeness of gospel grace plead an indulgence for sin.

Manner of coming to God.—And now to speak a few words of coming to God, or coming as the text intends. And in speaking to this, I must touch upon two things—1. Concerning God. 2. Concerning the frame of the heart of him that comes to him.

1. Of God. God is the chief good. Good so as nothing is but himself. He is in himself most happy; yea, all good; and all true happiness is only to be found in God, as that which is essential to his nature; nor is there any good or any happiness in or with any creature or thing but what is communicated to it by God. God is the only desirable good, nothing without him is worthy of our hearts. Right thoughts of God are able to ravish the heart; how much more happy is the man that has interest in God. God alone is able by himself to put the soul into a more blessed, comfortable, and happy condition than can the whole world; yea, and more than if all the created happiness of all the angels of heaven did dwell in one man's bosom. God is the upholder of all creatures, and whatever they have that is a suitable good to their

1 There has been, in every age, professors who, instead of gratefully receiving and obeying the *whole* truth, have indulged in favourite doctrines. Happy is that Christian who equally loves to hear Christ set forth as a priest and sacrifice, or to dwell upon his power and authority as king and lawgiver; who delights as much in holy obedience as in electing love. The saints are bound to bear with each other, never forgetting that they are members of one family, and must cherish and comfort one another, as we hope to enjoy fellowship with heaven and the smiles of the great Head of the church.—OFFOR.
2 Matthew 5:8.

kind, it is from God; by God all things have their subsistence, and all the good that they enjoy. I cannot tell what to say; I am drowned! The life, the glory, the blessedness, the soul-satisfying goodness that is in God is beyond all expression.

2. Now there must be in us something of a suitableness of spirit to this God before we can be willing to come to him.

Before, therefore, God has been with a man, and has left some impression of his glory upon him, that man cannot be willing to come to him aright. Hence it is said concerning Abraham, that, in order to his coming to God, and following of him aright, the Lord himself did show himself unto him—'Men, brethren, and fathers, hearken; The God of glory appeared unto our father Abraham, when he was in Mesopotamia, before he dwelt in Charran, and said unto him, Get thee out of thy country, and from thy kindred, and come into the land which I shall show thee.'[1]

It was this God of glory, the sight and visions of this God of glory, that provoked Abraham to leave his country and kindred to come after God. The reason why men are so careless of, and so indifferent about, their coming to God, is because they have their eyes blinded, because they do not perceive his glory. God is so blessed a one, that did he not hide himself and his glory, the whole world would be ravished with him. But he has, I will not say reasons of state, but reasons of glory, glorious reasons why he hideth himself from the world, and appeareth but to particular ones. Now by his thus appearing to Abraham, down fell Abraham's vanity, and his idolatrous fancies and affections, and his heart began to turn unto God, for that there was in this appearance an alluring and soul-instructing voice. Hence that which Moses calls here an *appearing*, Christ calls a *hearing*, and a *teaching*, and a *learning*—'It is written in the prophets, And they shall be all taught of God. Every man, therefore, that hath heard and hath learned of the Father, cometh unto me,' that is, to God by me. But, I say, what must they hear and learn of the Father but that Christ is the way to glory, the way to the God of glory. This is a drawing

1 Acts 7:2–3; Genesis 12:1.

doctrine; wherefore that which in this verse is called *teaching* and *learning*, is called, in the verse before, the *drawing* of the Father— 'No man can come to me except the Father which hath sent me draw him;' that is, with powerful proposals, and alluring conclusions, and heart-subduing influences.[1]

Having thus touched upon this, we will now proceed to show you what kind of people they are that come to God by Christ; and then shall draw some inferences from this also.

WHO ARE THE PEOPLE THAT COME TO CHRIST

There are, therefore, three sorts of people that come to God by Christ. *First*, Men newly awakened. *Second*, Men turned from backsliding. *Third*, The sincere and upright man.

Of the newly awakened coming to Christ

First, Men newly awakened. By awakened, I mean awakened thoroughly. So awakened as to be made to see themselves, what they are; the world, what it is; the law, what it is; hell, what it is; death, what it is; Christ, what he is; and God, what he is; and also what judgment is.

A man that will come to God by Christ aright must needs, precedent to his so coming, have a competent knowledge of things of this kind.

1. He must know himself, *what a wretched and miserable sinner he is*, before he will take one step forward in order to his coming to God by Christ. This is plain from a great many scriptures; as that of the parable of the prodigal,[2] that of the three thousand,[3] that of the jailer,[4] and those of many more besides. The whole have no need of the physician. They were not the sound and whole, but the lame and

---

1 John 6:44–45.
2 Luke 15.
3 Acts 2.
4 Acts 16.

diseased that came to him to be cured of their infirmities; and it is
not the righteous, but the sinners that do well know themselves to be
such, that come to God by Christ.

It is not in the power of all the men on earth to make one man
come to God by Christ, because it is not in their power to make men
see their state by nature. And what should a man come to God for,
that can live in the world without him? Reason says so, experience says
so, the Scripture beareth witness that so it is of a truth. It is a sight of
what I am that must *unroost* me, that must shake my soul, and make
me leave my present rest. No man comes to God by Christ but he that
knows himself, and what sin hath done to him; that is the first.[1]

2. As he must know himself, and what a wretch he is, so *he must
know the world, and what an empty thing it is.* Cain did see himself, but saw not the emptiness of this world; and therefore instead
of going to God by Christ, he went to the world, and there did take
up to his dying day.[2] The world is a great snare to the soul, even to
the souls of awakened sinners, by reason of its big looks, and the fair
promises that it makes to those that will please to entertain it. It will
also make as though it could do as much to the quieting of the spirit
as either sermon, Bible, or preacher. Yea, and it has its followers ready
at its heels continually to blow its applause abroad, saying, 'Who
will show us *any* (other) good?'[3] And though 'this their way *is* their
folly: yet their posterity approve their sayings.'[4] So that unless a man,
under some awakenings, sees the emptiness of the world, he will take
up in the good things thereof, and not come to God by Christ. Many
there be now in hell that can seal to this for truth. It was the world
that took awakened Cain, awakened Judas, awakened Demas. Yea,
Balaam, though he had some kind of visions of God, yet was kept by
the world from coming to him aright. See with what earnestness the
young man in the gospel came to Jesus Christ, and that for eternal
life. He ran to him, he kneeled down to him, and asked, and that

1 Job 21:7–15.
2 Genesis 4:16.
3 Psalm 4:6.
4 Psalm 49:13.

before a multitude, 'Good master, what shall I do that I may inherit eternal life?'[1] And yet when he was told he could not come, the world soon stepped betwixt that life and him, and persuaded him to take up in itself; and so, for aught we know, he never looked after life more.

There are four things in the world that have a tendency to lull an awakened man asleep, if God also makes him not afraid of the world.

(1.) There is the bustle and cumber of the world, that will call a man off from looking after the salvation of his soul. This is intimated by the parable of the thorny ground.[2] Worldly cumber is a devilish thing; it will hurry a man from his bed without prayer; to a sermon, and from it again, without prayer; it will choke prayer, it will choke the Word, it will choke convictions, it will choke the soul, and cause that awakening shall be to no saving purpose.

(2.) There is the friendship of this world, to which, if a man is not mortified, there is no coming for him to God by Christ. And a man can never be mortified to it unless he shall see the emptiness and vanity of it. Whosoever makes himself a friend of this world is the enemy of God. And how, then, can he come to him by Christ?[3]

(3.) There are the terrors of the world, if a man stands in fear of them, he also will not come to God by Christ. The fear of man brings a snare. How many have, in all ages, been kept from coming to God aright by the terrors of the world? Yea, how many are there to one's thinking have almost got to the gates of heaven, and have been scared and driven quite back again by nothing but the terrors of this world? This is that which Christ so cautioneth his disciples about, for he knew it was a deadly thing. Peter also bids the saints beware of this as of a thing very destructive.[4]

(4.) There is also the glory of the world, an absolute hindrance to convictions and awakenings, to wit, honours, and greatness, and preferments: 'How can ye believe,' said Christ, 'which receive honour one of another, and seek not the honour that *cometh* from God

1 Mark 10:17–24.
2 Luke 8:14.
3 James 4:4.
4 Luke 12:4–6; 1 Peter 3:14–15.

THE PERSONS INTERESTED IN THIS INTERCESSION   59

only.'[1] If therefore a man is not in his affections crucified to these, it will keep him from coming to God aright.

3. As a man must know himself, how vile he is, and know the world, how empty it is, so *he must know the law, how severe it is;* else he will not come to God by Jesus Christ our Lord.

A man that is under awakenings, is under a double danger of falling short of coming to God by Christ. If he knows not the severity of the law, he is either in danger of slighting its penalty, or of seeking to make amends to it by doing of good works; and nothing can keep him from splitting his soul upon one of these two rocks, but a sound knowledge of the severity of the law.

(1.) He is in danger of slighting the penalty. This is seen by the practice of all the profane in the world. Do they not know the law? Verily, many of them can say the Ten Commandments without book. But they do not know the severity of the law; and therefore when at any time awakenings come upon their consciences, they strive to drive away the guilt of one sin, by wallowing in the filth of another.

But would they do thus if they knew the severity of the law? they would as soon eat fire. The severity of the law would be an intolerable, insupportable burden to their consciences; it would drive them, and make them fly for refuge, to lay hold on the hope set before them.

(2.) Or if he slights not the penalty, he will seek to make amends to it by doing of good works for the sins he has committed. This is manifest by the practice of the Jews and Turks, and all that swerve on that hand—to wit, to seek life and happiness by the law. Paul also was here before he met with Jesus in the way. This is natural to consciences that are awakened, unless also they have given to them to see the true severity of the law; the which that thou mayest do, if my mite will help, I will cast in for thy conviction these four things—

(*a.*) The law charges thee with its curse, as well for the pollution of thy nature, as for the defilements of thy life; yea, and if thou hadst never committed sinful act, thy pollution of nature must stand in thy way to life, if thou comest not to God for mercy by Christ.

---

1 John 5:44.

(*b.*) The law takes notice of, and chargeth thee with its curse, as well for sinful thoughts as for vile and sinful actions. 'The (very) thought of foolishness *is* sin,'[1] though it never breaks out into act, and will as surely merit the damnation of the soul as will the greatest transgression in the world.

(*c.*) If now thou couldst keep all the commandments, that will do thee no good at all, because thou hast sinned first: 'The soul that sinneth shall die.' Unless, then, thou canst endure the curse, and so in a legal way overcome it for the sins that thou hast committed, thou art gone, if thou comest not to God by Christ for mercy and pardon.

(*d.*) And never think of repentance, thereby to stop the mouth of the law; for the law calleth not for repentance, but life; nor will it accept of any, shouldst thou mourn and weep for thy sins till thou hast made a sea of blood with tears. This, I say, thou must know, or thou wilt not come to God by Christ for life. For the knowledge of this will cause that thou shalt neither slight the severity of the law, nor trust to the works thereof for life. Now, when thou doest neither of these, thou canst not but speed thee to God by Christ for life; for now thou hast no stay; pleasures are gone, all hope in thyself is gone. Thou now diest, and that is the way to live; for this inward death is, or feels like, a hunger-bitten stomach, that cannot but crave and gape for meat and drink. Now it will be as possible for thee to sleep with thy finger in the fire, as to forbear craving of mercy so long as this knowledge remains.

4. As a man must know himself, the emptiness of this world, and the law, so *it is necessary for him to know that there is a hell, and how insupportable the torments of it are;* for all threatenings, curses, and determinations to punish in the next world will prove but fictions and scarecrows, if there be no woful place, no woful state, for the sinner to receive his wages in for sin, when his days are ended in this world. Wherefore, this word 'saved' supposeth such a place and state. He is able to save from hell, from the woful place, from the woful state of hell, them that come unto God by him.

Christ, therefore, often insinuates the truth of a hell in his

1 Proverbs 24:9.

invitations to the sinners of this world to come to him; as where he tells them they shall be saved if they do, they shall be damned if they do not. As if he had said, there is a hell, a terrible hell, and they that come to me I will save them from it; but they that come not, the law will damn them in it. Therefore, that thou mayest indeed come to God by Christ for mercy, believe there is a hell, a woful, terrible place. Hell is God's creature, 'he hath made it deep and large!' The punishments are by the lashes of his wrath, which will issue from his mouth like a stream of burning brimstone, ever kindling itself upon the soul.[1] Thou must know this by the Word, and fly from it, or thou shalt know it by thy sins, and lie and cry in it.

I might enlarge, but if I did, I should be swallowed up; for we are while here no more able to set forth the torments of hell, than we are while here to set forth the joys of heaven; only this may, and ought to be said, that God is able, as to save, so to cast into hell.[2] And as he is able to make heaven sweet, good, pleasurable, and glorious beyond thought; so he is able to make the torments of hell so exquisite, so hot, so sharp, so intolerable, that no tongue can utter it, no, not the damned in hell themselves.[3] If thou lovest thy soul, slight not the knowledge of hell, for that, with the law, are the spurs which Christ useth to prick souls forward to himself withal. What is the cause that sinners can play so delightfully with sin? It is for that they forget there is a hell for them to descend into for their so doing, when they go out of this world. For here usually he gives our stop to a sinful course; we perceive that hell hath opened her mouth before us. Lest thou shouldst forget, I beseech thee, another time, to retain the knowledge of hell in thine understanding, and apply the burning-hot thoughts thereof to thy conscience; this is one way to make thee gather up thy heels, and mend thy pace in thy coming to Jesus Christ, and to God the Father by him.[4]

---

1 Isaiah 30:33.

2 Luke 12:5.

3 Isaiah 64:4.

4 Nothing can be more solemn and awful than are these warnings. O that we may feel the spurs, the condemning curse of a broken law, and a sense of the jaws of hell, urging us on in coming to, and cleaving to Christ.—OFFOR.

5. It is also necessary that he that cometh to God by the Lord Jesus, should know *what death is, and the uncertainty of its approaches upon us.* Death is, as I may call it, the feller, the cutter down. Death is that that puts a stop to a further living here, and that which lays man where judgment finds him. If he is in the faith in Jesus, it lays him down there to sleep till the Lord comes; if he be not in the faith, it lays him down in his sins till the Lord comes.[1] Again; if thou hast some beginnings that look like good, and death should overtake thee before those beginnings are ripe, thy fruit will wither, and thou wilt fall short of being gathered into God's barn. Some men are 'cut off as the tops of the ears of corn,' and some are even nipped by death in the very bud of their spring; but the safety is when a man is ripe, and shall be gathered to his grave, as a shock of corn to the barn in its season.[2]

Now if death should surprise and seize thee before thou art fit to die, all is lost; for there is no repentance in the grave, or rather, as the wise man has it, 'Whatsoever thy hand findeth to do, do *it* with thy might: for *there is* no work, nor device, nor knowledge, nor wisdom, in the grave, whither thou goest.'[3]

Death is God's sergeant, God's bailiff, and he arrests in God's name when he comes, but seldom gives warning before he clappeth us on the shoulder; and when he arrests us, though he may stay a little while, and give us leave to pant, and tumble, and toss ourselves for a while upon a bed of languishing, yet at last he will prick our bladder, and let out our life, and then our soul will be poured upon the ground, yea, into hell, if we are not ready and prepared for the life everlasting. He that doth not watch for, and is not afraid lest death should prevent him, will not make haste to God by Christ. What Job said of temporal afflictions, such an one will death be if thou art not aware—'When I looked for good, then evil came . . . The days of affliction prevented me.'[4] If thou lookest, or beginnest to look for good, and the day of death shall cut thee off before thou hast found

1 Hebrews 11:13; 1 Thessalonians 4:14; Job 20:11.
2 Job 24:20–24; 5:26.
3 Ecclesiastes 9:10.
4 Job 30:26–27.

that good thou lookest for, all is lost, soul, and life, and heaven, and all. Wherefore it is convenient that thou conclude the grave is thy house, and that thou make thy bed once a day in the grave; also that thou say unto corruption, 'Thou *art* my father; to the worm, *thou art* my mother and my sister.'[1] I say, be acquainted with the grave and death. The fool puts the evil day far away, but the wise man brings it nigh. Better be ready to die seven years before death comes, than want one day, one hour, one moment, one tear, one sorrowful sigh at the remembrance of the ill-spent life that I have lived. This, then, is that which I admonish thee of; namely, that thou know death, what it is, what it doth when it comes. Also, that thou consider well of the danger that death leaves that man in, to whom he comes before he is ready and prepared to be laid by it in the grave.

6. Thou must also be made by thy awakenings *to see what Christ is*. This is of absolute necessity; for how can or shall a man be willing to come to Christ that knows not what he is, what God has appointed him to do? He is the Saviour, every man will say so; but to sense, smell, and taste, what saving is, and so to understand the nature of the office and work of a Saviour, is a rare thing, kept close from most, known but by some. Jesus of Nazareth is the Saviour or the reconciler of men to God in the body of his flesh through death.[2] This is he whose business in coming from heaven to earth was to save his people from their sins. Now, as was said, to know how he doth this, is that which is needful to be inquired into; for some say he doth it one way, some, he doth it another; and it must be remembered that we are now speaking of the salvation of that man that from new or first awakenings, is coming to God by Christ for life. (1.) Some say he doth it, by giving of us precepts and laws to keep, that we might be justified thereby. (2.) Some say that he doth it, by setting himself a pattern for us to follow him. (3.) Some again hold, that he doth it by our following the light within.

But thou must take heed of all these, for he justifies us by none

---

1 Job 17:13–14.
2 Colossians 1:19–21.

of these means, and thou dost need to be justified. I say, he justifieth us, not either by giving laws unto us, or by becoming our example, or by our following of him in any sense, but by his blood shed for us. His blood is not laws, nor ordinances, nor commandments, but a price, a redeeming price.[1] He justifies us by bestowing upon us, not by expecting from us; he justifies us by his grace, not by our works.[2] In a word, thou must be well grounded in the knowledge of what Christ is, and how men are justified by him, or thou wilt not come unto God by him.

As thou must know him, and how men are justified by him, so thou must know the readiness that is in him to receive and to do for those what they need that come unto God by him. Suppose his merits were never so efficacious, yet if it could be proved that there is a loathness in him that these merits should be bestowed upon the coming ones, there would but few adventure to wait upon him. But now, as he is full, he is free. Nothing pleases him better than to give what he has away; than to bestow it upon the poor and needy. And it will be convenient that thou who art a coming soul shouldst know this for thy comfort to encourage thee to come to God by him. Take two or three sayings of his, for the confirming of what is now said. 'Come unto me, all *ye* that labour and are heavy laden, and I will give you rest.'[3] 'All that the Father giveth me shall come to me; and him that cometh to me I will in no wise cast out.'[4] 'I came not to call the righteous, but sinners to repentance.'[5] 'This *is* a faithful saying, and worthy of all acceptation, that Christ Jesus came into the world to save sinners; of whom I am chief.'[6]

7. As a man that would come to God by Christ must, antecedent to his so coming, know himself, what he is; the world, how empty it is; the law, how severe it is; death, and what it is; and Christ, and

---

1 Romans 5:7–9; Revelation 1:5.
2 Ephesians 1:7.
3 Matthew 11:28.
4 John 6:37.
5 Mark 2:17.
6 1 Timothy 1:15.

what he is; *so also he must know God.* 'He that cometh to God must believe that he is, and *that* he is a rewarder of them that diligently seek him.'[1] God must be known, else how can the sinner propound him as his end, his ultimate end? For so doth every one that indeed doth come to Christ aright; he comes to Christ because he is the way; he comes to God because he is the end. But, I say, if he knows him not, how can he propound him as the end? The end is that for the sake of which I propound to myself anything, and for the sake of which I use any means. Now, then, I would be saved; but why? Even because I would enjoy God. I use the means to be saved; and why? Because I would enjoy God. I am sensible that sin has made me come short of the glory of God, and that Christ Jesus is he, the only he, that can put me into a condition of obtaining the glory of God; and, therefore, I come to God by him.[2]

But, I say again, who will propound God for his end that knows him not, that knows him not aright? yea, that knows him not, to be worth being propounded as my end in coming to Jesus Christ; and he that thus knows him must know him to be above all, best of all, and him in whom the soul shall find that content, that bliss, that glory and happiness that can by no means be found elsewhere. And, I say, if this be not found in God, the soul will never propound him to itself as the only, highest, and ultimate end in its coming to Jesus Christ. But it will propound something else, even what it shall imagine to be the best good; perhaps heaven, perhaps ease from guilt, perhaps to be kept out of hell, or the like. I do not say but a man may propound all these to himself, in his coming to Jesus Christ; but if he propound these as his ultimate end, as the chiefest good that he seeks; if the presence and enjoyment of God, of God's glorious majesty, be not his chief design, he is not concerned in the salvation that is propounded in our text—'He is able,' and so will 'save to the uttermost them that come unto God by him.'

What is heaven without God? what is ease without the peace and

1 Hebrews 11:6.
2 Romans 3:23; 5:1–2.

enjoyment of God? what is deliverance from hell without the enjoyment of God? The propounding, therefore, these, and only these, to thyself for thy happiness in thy coming to Jesus Christ is a proposal not a hair's breadth higher than what a man without grace can propound. What or who is he that would not go to heaven? What or who is he that would not also have ease from the guilt of sin? And where is the man that chooseth to go to hell? But many there be that cannot abide God; no, they like not to go to heaven, because God is there. If the devil had a heaven to bestow upon men, a vicious and a beastly heaven, if it be lawful thus to speak, I durst pawn my soul upon it, were it a thousand times better than it is, that, upon a bare invitation, the foul fiend would have twenty to God's one. They, I say, cannot abide God; nay, for all, the devil has nothing but a hell for them; yet how thick men go to him, but how thinly to God Almighty. The nature of God lieth cross to the lusts of men. A holy God, a glorious holy God, an infinitely holy God, this spoils all. But to the soul that is awakened, and that is made to see things as they are; to him God is what he is in himself, the blessed, the highest, the only eternal good, and he without the enjoyment of whom all things would sound but emptily in the ears of that soul.

Now, then, I advise thee that hast a mind to come to God by Christ, that thou seek the knowledge of God—'If thou seekest wisdom as silver, and searchest for her as *for* hid treasures, then shalt thou understand the fear of the Lord, and find the knowledge of God.'[1] And to encourage thee yet further, he is so desirous of communion with men, that he pardoneth sins for that. Hence he is called not only loving, but love. 'God is love; and he that dwelleth in love dwelleth in God, and God in him.'[2]

Methinks, when I consider what glory there is at times upon the creatures, and that all their glory is the workmanship of God; O Lord, say I, what is God himself? He may well be called the God of glory, as well as the glorious Lord; for as all glory is from him, so in him is

1 Proverbs 2:4–5.
2 1 John 4:16.

an inconceivable well-spring of glory, of glory to be communicated to them that come by Christ to him. Wherefore, let the glory, and love, and bliss, and eternal happiness that is in God allure thee to come to him by Christ.

8. As thou shouldst, nay, must, have a good knowledge of all these, *so thou must have it of judgment to come.* They that come to God by Christ are said to 'flee from the wrath to come;' to 'flee for refuge, to lay hold on the hope set before them.'[1]

This judgment to come is a warm thing to be thought of, an awakening thing to be thought of; it is called the eternal judgment, because it is and will be God's final conclusion with men. This day is called the 'great and notable day of the Lord,'[2] the day 'that shall burn like an oven,'[3] the day in which the angels shall gather the wicked together, as tares, into bundles, to burn them; but the rest, into his kingdom and glory. This day will be it in which all the bowels of love and compassion shall be shut up to the wicked, and that in which the floodgates of wrath shall be opened, by which shall a plentiful reward be given to evil-doers, but glory to the righteous.[4] This is the day in which men, if they could, would creep into the ground for fear; but because they cannot, therefore, they will call and cry to the mountains to fall upon them, but they shall not; therefore, they stand bound to bear their judgment.

This day will be the day of breaking up of closet-councils, cabinet-councils, secret purposes, hidden thoughts; yea, 'God shall bring every work into judgment, with every secret thing.'[5] I say he shall do it then; for he will both 'bring to light the hidden things of darkness, and will make manifest the counsels of the heart.'[6] This is the day that is appointed to put them to shame and contempt in that have, in this world, been bold and audacious in their vile and beastly ways. At this

1 Matthew 3:7; Hebrews 6:18.
2 Acts 2:20.
3 Malachi 4:1.
4 Psalm 31:23.
5 Ecclesiastes 12:14.
6 1 Corinthians 4:5.

day, God will cover all such bold and brazen faces with shame. Now
they will blush till the blood is ready to burst through their cheeks.[1]
Oh! the confusion and shame that will cover their faces while God is
discovering to them what a nasty, what a beastly, what an uncomely,
and what an unreasonable life they lived in the world. They shall now
see they contemned God, that fed them, that clothed them, that gave
them life and limb, and that maintained their breath in their nostrils.
But, oh, when they see the gulf before them, and all things ready
to receive them in thither; then, then they will know what sinning
against God means!

And, I say, thou that art for coming to God by Christ must know
this, and be well assured of this, or thou wilt never come to God by
him.

What of the glory of God shall be put upon them that do indeed
come to him will also help in this spiritual journey, if it be well considered by thee. But, perhaps, terror and unbelief will suffer thee to
consider but little of that. However, the things afore-mentioned will
be goads, and will serve to prick thee forward; and if they do so, they
will be God's great blessing unto thee, and that for which thou wilt
give him thy thanks for ever.[2]

Thus I have, in few words, spoken something as to the first sort
of comers to God by Christ, namely, of the coming of the newly-
awakened man. And I say again, if any of the things afore-named be
wanting, and are not with his heart, it is a question whether, notwithstanding all the noise that he may make about religion, he will ever
come to God by Christ.

1. If he knows not himself and the badness of his condition,
wherefore should he come?

2. If he knows not the world, and the emptiness and vanity
thereof, wherefore should he come?

3. If he knows not the law, and the severity thereof, wherefore
should he come?

---

1 David 12:2.
2 Ecclesiastes 12:10–11.

4. If he knows not hell, and the torments thereof, wherefore should he come?

5. If he knows not what death is, wherefore should he come?

6. And if he knows not the Father and the Son, how can he come?

7. And to know that there is a judgment to come is as necessary to his coming as most of the rest of the things propounded.

Coming to God by Christ is for shelter, for safety, for advantage, and everlasting happiness. But he that knows not, that understands not the things afore-mentioned, sees not his need of taking shelter, of flying for safety, of coming for advantage to God by Christ. I know there are degrees of this knowledge, and he that has it most warm upon him, in all likelihood, will make most haste; or, as David saith, will hasten his escape 'from the windy storm and tempest;' and he that sees least is in most danger of being the loiterer, and so of losing the prize; for all that run do not obtain it; all that fight do not win it; and ALL that strive for it have it not.[1]

Of the backslider's return to Christ

Second, I shall now come to the second man mentioned; to wit, *the man that is turning back from his backsliding*, and speak something also about his coming again to God by Christ.

There are two things remarkable in the returning of a backslider to God by Christ. 1. The first is, he gives a second testimony to the truth of all things spoken of before. 2. He also gives a second testimony of the necessity of coming to God by Christ. Of the manner of his coming to God by Christ perhaps I may also speak a word or two. But,

1. The returning again of the backslider gives a second testimony to the truth of man's state being by nature miserable, of the vanity of this world, of the severity of the law, certainty of death, and terribleness of judgment to come. His first coming told them so, but his second coming tells them so with a double confirmation of the

1 Psalm 55:8; 1 Corinthians 9:24–26; 2 Timothy 2:4–5.

truth. It is so, saith his first coming. Oh! it is so, saith his second. The backsliding of a Christian comes through the overmuch persuading of Satan and lust, that the man was mistaken, and that there was no such horror in the things from which he fled, nor so much good in the things to which he hasted. Turn again, fool, says the devil, turn again to thy former course; I wonder what frenzy it was that drove thee to thy heels, and that made thee leave so much good behind thee, as other men find in the lusts of the flesh and the good of the world. As for the law, and death, and an imagination of the day of judgment, they are but mere scarecrows, set up by politic heads, to keep the ignorant in subjection. Well, says the backslider, I will go back again and see; so, fool as he is, he goes back, and has all things ready to entertain him; his conscience sleeps, the world smiles, flesh is sweet, carnal company compliments him, and all that can be got is presented to this backslider to accommodate him. But, behold, he doth again begin to see his own nakedness, and he perceives that the law is whetting his axe. As for the world, he perceives it is a bubble; he also smells the smell of brimstone, for God hath scattered it upon his tabernacle, and it begins to burn within him.[1] Oh! saith he, I am deluded; oh! I am insnared. My first sight of things was true. I see it is so again. Now he begins to be for flying again to his first refuge; O God, saith he, I am undone, I have turned from thy truth to lies! I believed them such at first, and find them such at last. Have mercy upon me, O God!

This, I say, is a testimony, a second testimony, by the same man, as to the miserable state of man, the severity of the law, the emptiness of the world, the certainty of death, and the terribleness of judgment. This man hath seen it, and seen it again.

A returning backslider is a great blessing, I mean intended to be so, to two sorts of men—1. To the elect uncalled. 2. To the elect that are called, and that at present stand their ground. The uncalled are made to hear him, and consider; the called are made to hear him, and are afraid of falling. Behold, therefore, the mystery of God's wisdom,

---

1 Job 18:15.

and how willing he is that spectators should be warned and made take heed. Yea, he will permit that some of his own shall fall into the fire, to convince the world that hell is hot, and to warn their brethren to take heed that they slip not with their feet. I have often said in my heart that this was the cause why God suffered so many of the believing Jews to fall; to wit, that the Gentiles might take heed.[1] O, brethren! saith the backslider that is returned, did you see how I left my God? did you see how I turned again to those vanities from which some time before I fled? O! I was deluded, I was bewitched, I was deceived; for I found all things from which I fled at first still worse by far when I went to them the second time. Do not backslide. Oh! do not backslide. The *first* ground of your departing from them was good; never tempt God a second time.

2. And as he gives us a second testimony, that the world and himself are so as at first he believed they were, so by this his returning he testifies that God and Christ are the same, and much more than ever he believed at first they were. This man has made a proof before and a proof after conviction of the evil of the one and good of the other. This man has made a proof by feeling and seeing, and that before and after grace received. This man God has set up to be a witness; this man is two men, has the testimony of two men, must serve in the place of two men. He knows what it is to be fetched from a state of nature by grace; but this all Christians know as well as he. Ay, but he knows what it is to be fetched from the world, from the devil, and hell, the *second time;* and that but few professors know, for few that fall away return to God again.[2] Ay, but this man is come again, wherefore there is news in his mouth, sad news, dreadful news, and news that is to make the standing saint to take heed lest he fall. The returning backslider, therefore, is a rare man, a man of worth and intelligence, a man to whom the men of the world should flock, and of whom they should learn to fear the Lord God. He also is a man of whom the saints should receive both caution, counsel, and strength

1 Romans 11:21.
2 Hebrews 6:4–8.

in their present standing; and they should, by his harms, learn to serve the Lord with fear, and to rejoice with trembling.[1]

This man has the second time also had a proof of God's goodness in his Christ unto him, a proof which the standing Christian has not—I would not tempt him that stands to fall; but the good that a returning backslider has received at God's hands, and at the hand of Christ, is a double good, he has been converted twice, fetched from the world, and from the devil, and from himself twice; oh, grace! and has been made to know the stability of God's covenant, the unchangeableness of God's mind, the sure and lasting truth of his promise in Christ, and of the sufficiency of the merits of Christ, over and over.

The manner of a backslider's return.—Of the manner of this man's coming to God by Christ I shall also speak a word or two. He comes as the newly-awakened sinner comes, and that from the same motives and the knowledge of things as he hath over and above (which he had as good have been without), that which the newly-awakened sinner has not; to wit, the guilt of his backsliding, which is a guilt of a worse complexion, of a deeper dye, and of a heavier nature than is any guilt else in the world. He is also attended with fears and doubts that arise from other reasons and considerations than do the doubts and fears of the newly-awakened man; doubts builded upon the vileness of his backsliding. He has also more dreadful scriptures to consider of, and they will look more wishfully in his face, yea, and will also make him take notice of their grim physiognomy, than has the newly-awakened man. Besides, as a punishment of his backsliding, God seems to withdraw the sweet influences of his Spirit, and as if he would not suffer him to pray, nor to repent any more,[2] as if he would now take all away from him, and leave him to those lusts and idols that he left his God to follow. Swarms of his new rogueries shall haunt him in every place, and that not only in the guilt, but in the filth and pollution of them.[3] None know the things that haunt a backslider's mind,

---

1 1 Corinthians 10:6–13; Psalm 51:11–13; Luke 22:32.
2 Psalm 51:11.
3 Proverbs 14:14.

his *new* sins are all turned talking devils, threatening devils, roaring devils, within him. Besides, he doubts of the truth of his first conversion, consequently he has it lying upon him as a strong suspicion that there was nothing of truth in all his first experience; and this also adds *lead* to his heels, and makes him come, as to sense and feeling, more heavy and with the greater difficulty to God by Christ. As faithfulness of other men kills him, he cannot see an honest, humble, holy, faithful servant of God, but he is pierced and wounded at the heart. Ay, says he within himself, that man fears God, that man hath faithfully followed God, that man, like the elect angels, has kept his place; but I am fallen from my station like a devil. That man honoureth God, edifieth the saints, convinceth the world, and condemneth them, and is become heir of the righteousness which is by faith. But I have dishonoured God, stumbled and grieved saints, made the world blaspheme, and, for aught I know, been the cause of the damnation of many! These are the things, I say, together with many more of the same kind, that come with him; yea, they *will* come with him, yea, and will stare him in the face, will tell him of his baseness, and laugh him to scorn, all the way that he is coming to God by Christ—*I know what I say!*—and this makes his coming to God by Christ hard and difficult to him. Besides, he thinks saints will be aware of him, will be shy of him, will be afraid to trust him, yea, will tell his Father of him, and make intercession against him, as Elias did against Israel,[1] or as the men did that were fellow-servants with him that took his brother by the throat.[2] Shame covereth his face all the way he comes; he doth not know what to do; the God he is returning to, is the God that he has slighted, the God before whom he has preferred the vilest lust; and he knows God knows it, and has before him all his ways. The man that has been a backslider, and is returning to God, can tell strange stories, and yet such as are very true. No man was in the whale's belly, and came out again alive, but backsliding and returning Jonah; consequently, no man could tell how he was there, what he felt there, what he saw there, and what

1 Romans 11:2.
2 Matthew 18:31.

workings of heart he had when he was there, so well as he.

The sincere Christian's coming to God by Christ

Third, I come now to the third man—to wit, *to the sincere and upright man that cometh to God by Christ*. And although this may, in some sense, be applicable to the two former, for his coming is not worthy to be counted coming to God, that is, not in sincerity and uprightness, yet by such an one I now mean, one that has been called to the faith, and that has in some good measure of sincerity and uprightness therein abode with God.

This man also comes to God by Christ; but his coming is to be distinguished, I mean in the main of it, from the coming of the other two. The other come for the *knowledge* of forgiveness, a thing that the upright and faithful Christian for the most part has a comfortable faith of, and that for which he is often helped to give thanks to God. I do not say he doubteth not, or that he has not his evidences sometimes clouded; nor do I say that the knowledge of his reconciliation to God by Christ Jesus is so high, so firm, so fixed, and steadfast, that it cannot be shaken, or that he needs no more. I will then explain myself. He comes not to God as an unconverted sinner comes; he comes not as a backslider comes when he is returning to God from his backslidings; but he comes as a son, as one of the household of God, and he comes as one that has not, since correction, wickedly departed from his God.

1. He then comes to God with that access and godly boldness that is only proper to such as himself, that is, to them that walk with God.[1] Thus every one that shall be saved doth not do; thus every one that shall be saved cannot do—to instance the two spoken of before.

2. He comes to God by Christ constantly by prayer, by meditation, by every ordinance. For therefore he maketh use of ordinances, because by them through Christ he getteth into the presence of God.[2]

3. He comes to God through Christ, because he judgeth that God

---

1 Romans 5:2.
2 Psalm 27:4.

only is that good, that blessedness, that happiness, that is worth looking after; that good and that blessedness that alone can fill the soul to
the brim; that good and that happiness that is worthy of our hearts
and souls and spirits. Hence David expresseth his coming to God by
panting, by thirsting, by tears, saying, 'My soul panteth after thee,
O God.' And again, 'My soul thirsteth for God, for the living God,
when shall I come and appear before God?'[1] And again, 'I will go to
the altar of God, unto God, my exceeding joy.'[2] And hence it was that
he so envied the swallow and sparrow, even because they could come
to the altar of God, where he had promised to give his presence, when
he, as I think, by the rage of Saul, was forced to abide remote. 'My
soul longeth,' saith he, 'yea, even fainteth for the courts of the Lord;
my heart and my flesh crieth out for the living God. Yea, the sparrow
hath found a house, and the swallow a nest for herself, where she may
lay her young, *even* thine altars, O Lord of hosts, my King, and my
God. Blessed *are* they that dwell in thy house, they will be still praising
thee.' Then after a few more words he saith, 'For a day in thy courts is
better than a thousand. I had rather be a doorkeeper,' I would choose
rather to sit at the threshold of thy house, 'than to dwell in the tents of
wickedness;' and then renders the reason—'For the Lord *is* a sun and
shield: the Lord gives grace and glory,' etc.[3]

The presence of God, and the glory and soul-ravishing goodness
of that presence, is a thing that the world understands not, nor can
they *as such* desire to know what it is.

4. These good men come to God upon other accounts also; for so
it is that they have many concerns with God.

Concern for themselves.—(1.) They come to him for a more clear
discovery of themselves to themselves, for they desire to know how
frail they are, because the more they know that, the more they are
engaged in their souls to take heed to their ways, and to fear lest they
should tempt their God to leave them.[4]

1 Psalm 42:1–2.
2 Psalm 43:4.
3 Psalm 84.
4 Psalm 39:1–8.

(2.) They come to God by Christ for the weakening of their lusts and corruptions; for they are a sore, yea, a plague to a truly sanctified soul. Those, to be rid of which, if it might be, a godly man chooseth rather to die than to live. This David did mean when he cried, 'Create in me a clean heart, O God, and renew a right spirit within me,'[1] and Paul, when he cried out, 'O wretched man that I am, who shall deliver me from the body of this death?'[2]

(3.) They come to God by Christ for the renewing and strengthening of their graces. The graces that the godly have received are, and they feel they are, subject to decay; yea, they cannot live without a continual supply of grace. This is the meaning of that, 'Let us have grace,' and, 'Let us therefore come boldly unto the throne of grace, that we may obtain mercy, and find grace to help in time of need.'[3]

(4.) They come to God by Christ to be helped against those temptations that they may meet withal.[4] They know that every new temptation has a new snare and a new evil in it; but what snare and what evil, that at present they know not; but they know their God knows, and can deliver out of temptation when we are in, and keep us out while we are out.

(5.) They come to God by Christ for a blessing upon that means of grace which God has afforded for the succour of the soul, and the building of it up in the faith; knowing that as the means, so a blessing upon it, is from God.[5] And for this they have encouragement, because God has said, 'I will abundantly bless her provision: I will satisfy her poor with bread.'[6]

(6.) They come to God by Christ for the forgiveness of daily infirmities,[7] and for the continuing them in the light of his countenance notwithstanding. Thus he also would always accept them and their services, and grant that an answer of peace may be returned

1 Psalm 51:10.
2 Romans 7:24.
3 Hebrews 4:16.
4 Matthew 6:13.
5 2 Thessalonians 3:1.
6 Psalm 132:15.
7 Psalm 19:12.

from their Father into their bosoms; for this is the life of their souls. There are a great many such things that the sincere and upright man comes to God for, too many here to mention. But again,

Concern for the church and others.—(1.) This man also comes to God to beseech him for the flourishing of Christ's kingdom, which he knows will never be until Antichrist is dead, and till the Spirit be more plentifully poured upon us from on high. Therefore he also cries to God for the downfall of the first, and for the pouring out of the other.

(2.) He comes to God for the hastening the gathering in of his elect; for it is an affliction to him to think that so many of those for whom Christ died should be still in a posture of hostility against him.[1]

(3.) He comes to God for a spirit of unity to be poured out among believers, for, for the divisions of Reuben he has great thoughts of heart.

(4.) He comes to God to pray for magistrates, and that God would make speed to set them all to that work that is so desirable to his church—that is, to 'hate the whore,' 'to eat her flesh,' to 'make her desolate,' 'and burn her with fire.'[2]

(5.) He comes to God to beg that he would hasten that great and notable day, the day of the coming of our Lord Jesus, for he knows that Christ will never be exalted as he must be till then; yea, he also knows that God's church will never be as she would, and shall, till then.[3]

(6.) But the main meaning, if I may so call it, of this high text is this, that they that come to God by him—that is, by Christ, are those that come by Christ to God to enjoy him by faith and spirit here, and by open vision and unspeakable possession of him in the next world. This is the great design of the soul in its coming to God by Jesus Christ, and it comes to him by Jesus Christ because it dares not come by itself,

---

1 Psalm 122:6.
2 1 Timothy 2:1; Revelation 17:16.
3 Revelation 22:20.

and because God himself has made him the way, the new and living way. Here, as I said, the Father meets with that which pleaseth him, and the soul with that which saveth her. Here is righteousness and merits to spare, even righteousness that can justify the ungodly. Here is always, how empty soever we be, a fulness of merit always presented to God by Christ for my obtaining of that which at any time I want, whether wisdom, grace, Spirit, or any good thing soever; only, since I was upon this subject, I thought a little to touch upon things in this order, for the enlarging of thy thoughts, for the conviction of thy spirit, for the stirring of thee up to God, and for the showing of thee the good signs of grace where it is, where it is abused, and where any are seeking after it.

INFERENCES FROM THUS COMING TO GOD BY CHRIST

And now I come to draw some inferences from this point also, as I have already done from those going before it. You see that I have now been speaking to you of the man that cometh to God, both with respect to the way he comes, as also with respect to the manner of spirit in which he comes; and hence I may well infer,

First, That he is no fool, no fool according to the best judgment, that cometh to God by Christ. The world indeed will count him one; for the things that be of the Spirit of God are foolishness to them; but indeed, and in the verdict of true judgment, he is not so.

1. For that he now seeketh and intermeddleth with all wisdom. He has chosen to be concerned with the very head and fountain of wisdom; for Christ is the wisdom of God, and the way to the Father by Christ, is the greatest of mysteries; and to choose to walk in that way, the fruits of the most sage advice; wherefore he is not a fool that thus concerns himself.[1]

2. It is not a sign of foolishness timely to prevent ruin, is it? They are the prudent men that foresee an evil, and hide themselves; and the fools, that go on, and are punished.[2] Why, this man foresees an evil,

---

1 Proverbs 18:1; 1 Corinthians 1.
2 Proverbs 18:3; 27:12.

the greatest evil, sin, and the punishment of the soul for sin in hell; and flies to Christ, who is the refuge that God has provided for penitent sinners; and is this a sign of a fool? God make me such a fool, and thee that readest these lines such a fool, and then we shall be wiser than all men that are counted wise by the wisdom of this world. Is it a sign of a fool to agree with one's adversary while we are in the way with him, even before he delivereth us to the judge? Yea, it is a piece of the highest wisdom.

Is he a fool that chooseth for himself long lasters, or he whose best things will rot in a day? Sinners, 'before your pots can feel the thorns (before you can see where you are), God shall take you away as with a whirlwind, both living, and in *his* wrath.'[1] But this man has provided for things; like the tortoise, he has got a shell on his back, so strong and sound that he fears not to suffer a loaden cart to go over him. The Lord is his rock, his defence, his refuge, his high tower, unto which he doth continually resort.

Was the unjust steward a fool in providing for himself for hereafter? for providing friends to receive him to harbour when others should turn him out of their doors?[2] No more is he that gets another house for his harbour before death shall turn him out of doors here.

3. As he that cometh to God by Christ is no fool, so he is no little-spirited fellow. There are a generation of men in this world that count themselves men of the largest capacities, when yet the greatness of their desires lift themselves no higher than to things below. If they can, with their net of craft and policy, encompass a bulky lump of earth, oh what a treasure have they engrossed to themselves! Meanwhile, the man in the text has laid siege to heaven, has found out the way to get into the city, and is resolved, in and by God's help, to make that his own. Earth is a drossy thing in this man's account; earthly greatness and splendours are but like vanishing bubbles in this man's esteem. None but God, as the end of his desires, none but Christ, as the means to accomplish this his end, are things counted

1 Psalm 58:9.
2 Luke 16:8–9.

great by this man. No company now is acceptable to this man but the Spirit of God, Christ and angels, and saints, as fellow-heirs with himself. All other men and things he deals with as strangers and pilgrims were wont to do. This man's mind soars higher than the eagle or stork of the heavens. He is for musing about things that are above, and their glory, and for thinking what shall come to pass hereafter.

4. But as I have showed you what he is not, so now let me, by a few words, tell you what he is.

(1.) Then he is a man concerned for his soul, for his immortal soul. The soul is a thing, though of most worth, least minded by most. The souls of most lie waste while all other things are enclosed. But this man has got it by the end, that his soul is of more value than the world, wherefore he is concerned for his soul. Soul concerns are concerns of the highest nature, and concerns that arise from thoughts most deep and ponderous. He never yet knew what belonged to great and deep thoughts that is a stranger to soul concerns. Now the man that comes to God by Christ, is a man that is engaged in soul concerns.

(2.) He is a man whose spirit is subjected to a suitableness to spiritual things, for a carnal mind cannot suit with and be delighted in these things: 'The carnal mind *is* enmity against God; for it is not subject to the law of God, neither indeed can be.'[1] This is the man that God has tamed, and keeps tame by himself, while all other run wild, as the asses upon the mountains. If birds could speak, surely they would tell that those that are kept in the cage have with them another temper than they that range the air, and fly in the fields and woods. Yea, and could those kept tame express themselves to the rest, they would tell that they have white bread and milk, and sugar; while those without make a life out of maggots and worms. They are also in place where there are better things, and their companions are the children of men; besides, they learn such notes, and can whistle such tunes, as other birds are strangers to. Oh! the man whose spirit is subjected to God, betwixt whom and God there is a reconciliation, not only as to a difference made up, but also as to a oneness of heart; none

1 Romans 8:7.

knows what lumps of sugar God gives that man, nor what notes and tunes God learns that man: 'He hath put a new song in my mouth,' saith David, '*even* praise unto our God: many shall see *it*, and fear, and shall trust in the Lord.'[1]

Second. Is there a man that comes to God by Christ? Thence I infer that *there is that believes there is a world to come.* No man looks after that which yet he believes is not; faith must be before coming to Christ will be; coming is the fruit of faith. He that comes must believe antecedent to his coming; wherefore it is said, 'we walk by faith'—that is, we come to God through Christ by faith.[2] And hence I learn two things:—1. That faith is of a strong and forcible quality. 2. That they who come not to God by Christ have no faith.

1. Faith is of a strong and forcible quality, and that whether it be true or false.

(1.) A false faith has done great things; it has made men believe lies, plead for them, and stand to them, to the damnation of their souls. 'God shall send them strong delusion, that they should believe a lie,' to their damnation.[3] Hence it is said, men make lies 'their refuge.' Why? Because they 'trust in a lie.'[4] A lie, if believed, if a man has faith in it, it will do great things, because faith is of a forcible quality. Suppose thyself to be twenty miles from home, and there some man comes and possesses thee that thy house, thy wife and children, are all burned with the fire. If thou believest it, though indeed there should be nothing of truth in what thou hast heard, yet will this lie 'drink up thy spirit,' even as if the tidings were true. How many are there in the world whose heart Satan hath filled with a belief that their state and condition for another world is good? and these are made to live by lying hope that all shall be well with them, and so are kept from seeking for that which will make them happy indeed. Man is naturally apt and willing to be deceived, and therefore a groundless faith is the more taking and forcible. Fancy will help to confirm a false faith, and so will

1 Psalm 40:3.
2 Hebrews 11:7; 2 Corinthians 5:7.
3 2 Thessalonians 2:11–12.
4 Jeremiah 28:15.

conceit and idleness of spirit. There is also in man a willingness to take things upon trust, without searching into the ground and reason of them. Nor will Satan be behind hand to prompt and encourage to thy believing of a lie, for that he knows will be a means to bring thee to that end to which he greatly desireth thou shouldst come. Wherefore let men beware, and, oh, that they would, of a false and lying faith!

(2.) But if a false faith is so forcible, what is a true? What force, I say, is there in a faith that is begotten by truth, managed by truth, fed by truth, and preserved by the truth of God? This faith will make invisible things visible; not fantastically so, but substantially so— 'Now faith is the substance of things hoped for, the evidence of things not seen.'[1] True faith carrieth along with it an evidence of the certainty of what it believeth, and that evidence is the infallible Word of God. There is a God, a Christ, a heaven, saith the faith that is good, for the Word of God doth say so. The way to this God and this heaven is by Christ, for the Word of God doth say so. If I run not to this God by this Christ, this heaven shall never be my portion, for the Word of God doth say so. So, then, thus believing makes the man come to God by him. His thus believing, then, it is that carries him away from this world, that makes him trample upon this world, and that gives him the victory over this world. 'For whatsoever is born of God overcometh the world: and this is the victory that overcometh the world, *even* our faith. Who is he that evercometh the world, but he that believeth that Jesus is the Son of God? This is he that came by water and blood, *even* Jesus Christ; not by water only, but by water and blood. And it is the Spirit that beareth witness, because the Spirit is truth.'[2]

2. Now if this be true, that faith, true faith, is so forcible a thing as to take a man from his seat of ease, and make him to come to God by Christ as afore, then, is it not truly inferred from hence that they that come not to God by Christ have no faith. What! is man such a fool as to believe things, and yet not look after them? to believe great things, and yet not to concern himself with them? Who would knowingly go

1 Hebrews 11:1.
2 1 John 5:4–6.

over a pearl, and yet not count it worth stooping for? Believe thou art what thou art; believe hell is what it is; believe death and judgment are coming, as they are; and believe that the Father and the Son are, as by the Holy Ghost in the Word they are described, and sit still in thy sins if thou canst. Thou canst not sit still; faith is forcible. Faith is grounded upon the voice of God in the Word, upon the teaching of God in the Word. And it pleases God by the foolishness of preaching to save them that believe; for believing makes them heartily close in with, and embrace what by the Word is set before them, because it seeth the reality of them.

Shall God speak to man's soul, and shall not man believe? Shall man believe what God says, and nothing at all regard it? It cannot be. 'Faith comes by hearing, and hearing by the Word of God.' And we know that when faith is come, it purifies the heart of what is opposite to God, and the salvation of the soul.

So, then, those men that are at ease in a sinful course, or that come not to God by Christ, they are such as have no faith, and must therefore perish with the vile and unbelievers.[1]

The whole world is divided into two sorts of men—believers and unbelievers. The godly are called believers; and why believers, but because they are they that have given credit to the great things of the gospel of God? These believers are here in the text called also comers, or they that come to God by Christ, because whoso believes will come; for coming is a fruit of faith in the habit, or, if you will, it is faith in exercise; yet faith must have a being in the soul before the soul can put it into act.

This therefore further evidences that they that come not, have no faith, are not believers, belong not to the household of faith, and must perish—'For he that believes not, shall be damned.'

Nor will it be to any boot[2] to say, I believe there is a God and a

---

1 Revelation 21:8.
2 To any boot—to any profit.
        'What boots it at one gate to make defence,
        And at another to let in the foe?'
                Milton's *Samson Agonistes.*—OFFOR.

Christ, for still thy sitting still doth demonstrate that either thou liest in what thou sayest, or that thou believest with a worse than a false faith. But the object of my faith is true. I answer, so is the object of the faith of devils; for they believe that there is one God and one Christ, yet their faith, as to the root and exercise of it, is notwithstanding no such faith as is that faith that saves, or that is intended in the text, and that by which men come to God through Christ. Wherefore still, oh, thou slothful one, thou deceivest thyself! Thy not coming to God by Christ declareth to thy face that thy faith is not good, consequently, that thou feedest on ashes, and thy deceived heart has turned thee aside, that thou canst not deliver thy soul, nor say, '*Is there* not a lie in my right hand?'[1]

Third. Is there a man that comes to God by Christ? Thence I infer that *the world to come is better than this;* yea, so much better as to quit cost and bear charges of coming to God, from this, by Christ, to that. Though there is a world to come, yet if it were no better than this, one had as good stay here as seek that, or if it were better than this, and would bear charges if a man left this for that, and that was all, still the one would be as good as the other. But the man that comes to God by Christ, has chosen the world that is infinitely good; a world, betwixt which and this there can be no comparison. This must be granted, because he that comes to God by Christ is said to have made the best choice, even chose a city that has foundations.[2] There are several things that make it manifest enough that he that comes to God by Christ has made the best market, or chose the best world.

1. That is the world which God commendeth, but this that that he slighteth and contemneth.[3] Hence that is called the kingdom of God, but this an 'evil world.'[4] Now let us conclude, that since God made both, he is able to judge which of the two are best; yea, best able so to judge thereof. I choose the rather to refer you to the judgment

1 Isaiah 44:20.
2 Hebrews 11:10.
3 2 Thessalonians 1:5–6.
4 Galatians 1:4.

of God in this matter, for should I put you upon asking of him as
to this, that is, coming to God by Christ, perhaps you would say, he
is as little able to give an account of this matter as yourselves. But I
hope you think God knows, and therefore I refer you to the judgment
of God, which you have in the Scriptures of truth—'Heaven is his
throne, and the earth is his footstool.' I hope you will say here is some
difference. The Lord is the God of that, the devil the god and prince
of this. Thus also it appears there is some difference between them.

2. That world, and those that are counted worthy of it, shall all
be everlasting; but so shall not this, nor the inhabiters of it. The earth
with the works thereof shall be burned up, and the men that are of it
shall die in like manner.[1] '*But* Israel shall be saved in the Lord with an
everlasting salvation: ye shall not be ashamed nor confounded world
without end.'[2] This world, with the lovers of it, will end in a burning
hell; but the world to come fadeth not away.[3]

3. The world that we are now in, has its best comforts mixed
either with crosses or curses; but that to come with neither. There
shall be no more curse: and as for crosses, all tears shall be wiped from
the eyes of them that dwell there. There will be nothing but ravishing
pleasures, and holy; there will be no cessation of joys, nor any speck
of pollution. 'In thy presence *is* fullness of joy, at thy right hand *there
are* pleasures for evermore.'[4]

4. There men shall be made like angels, 'neither can they die any
more.'[5] There shall they behold the face of God and his Son, and
swim in the enjoyment of them for ever.

5. There men shall see themselves beyond all misery, and shall
know that it will be utterly impossible that either anything like sorrow, or grief, or sickness, or discontent, should touch them more.

6. There men shall be rewarded of God for what they have done
and suffered according to his will for his sake; there they shall eat and

1 2 Peter 3.
2 Isaiah 45:17.
3 1 Peter 1:3–4.
4 Psalm 16:11.
5 Luke 20:35–36.

drink their comforts, and wear them to their everlasting consolation.

7. They are all kings that go to that world, and so shall be proclaimed there. They shall also be crowned with crowns, and they shall wear crowns of life and glory, crowns of everlasting joy, crowns of lovingkindness; yea, 'In that day the Lord of hosts himself shall be for a crown of glory to those that are his people.'[1] Now, if this world, though no more could be said for it than is said in these few lines, is not infinitely far better than what the present world is, I have missed it in my thoughts. But the coming man, the man that comes to God by Christ, is satisfied, knows what he does; and if his way, all his way thither, were strewed with burning coals, he would choose, God helping him, to tread that path rather than to have his portion with them that perish.

Fourth, If there be a world to come, and such a way to it so safe and good, and if God is there to be enjoyed by them that come to him by Christ; *then this shows the great madness of the most of men*, madness, I say, of the highest degree, for that they come not to God by Christ that they may be inheritors of the world to come. It is a right character which Solomon gives of them, 'The heart,' saith he, 'of the sons of men is full of evil, and madness *is* in their heart while they live, and after that *they go* to the dead.'[2] A madman is intent upon his toys, upon anything but that about which he should be intent; and so are they that come not to God by Jesus Christ. A madman has neither ears to hear, nor a heart to do, what they that are in their right wits advise him for the best, no more have they that come not to God by Christ. A madman sets more by the straws and cock's feathers by which he decks himself, than he does by all the pearls and jewels in the world. And they that come not to God by Christ set more by the vanishing bubbles of this life than they do by that glory that the wise man shall inherit; 'The wise shall inherit glory, but shame,' says Solomon, 'shall be the promotion of fools.' What a shame it is to see God's jewels lie unregarded of them that yet think none are wiser than themselves.

---

1 Hebrews 2:7; Isaiah 28:5; 35:10; Psalm 103:4.
2 Ecclesiastes 9:3.

I know the wise men of this world will scorn one should think of them that they are mad; but verily it is so, the more wise for this world, the more fool in God's matters; and the more obstinately they stand in their way, the more mad. When Solomon gave himself to backsliding, he saith he gave himself to folly and madness.[1] And when he went about to search out what man is since the fall, he went about to search out foolishness and madness.[2] And is it not said, that when the Jews were angry with Jesus for that he did good on the Sabbath, that that anger did flow from their being filled with madness? Doth not Paul also, while he opposed himself against Christ, the gospel, and professors thereof, plainly tell us that he did it even from the highest pitch of madness? 'And being exceedingly mad against them, I persecuted *them* even unto strange cities.'[3] Now if it is exceeding madness to do thus, how many at this day must be counted exceeding mad, who yet count themselves the only sober men? They oppose themselves, they stand in their own light, they are against their own happiness, they cherish and nourish cockatrices in their own bosoms; they choose to themselves those paths which have written upon them in large characters, These are the ways of death and damnation. They are offended with them that endeavour to pull them out of their ditch, and choose rather to lie and die there than to go to God by Christ that they may be saved from wrath through him; yea, so mad are they, that they count the most sober, the most godly, the most holy man, the mad one; the more earnest for life, the more mad; the more in the Spirit, the more mad; the more desirous to promote the salvation of others, the more mad. But is not this a sign of madness, of madness unto perfection? And yet thus mad are many, and mad are all they that while it is called today, while their door is open, and while the golden sceptre of the golden grace of the blessed God is held forth, stand in their own light, and come not to God by Christ.[4] That is the fourth inference.

1 Ecclesiastes 1:17; 2:12.
2 Ecclesiastes 7:25–29.
3 Acts 26:11.
4 John 10:20; Acts 26:24.

Fifth, A fifth inference that I gather from this text is, *that the end that God will make with men will be according as they come or come not to God by Christ*. They that come to God by Christ have taken shelter and have hid themselves; but they that come not to God by Christ lay themselves open to the windy storm and tempest that will be in that day. And the wind then will be high, and the tempest strong, that will blow upon them that shall be found in themselves; 'Our God shall come, and shall not keep silence: a fire shall devour before him, and it shall be very tempestuous round about him. He shall call to the heavens from above, and to the earth, that he may judge his people.'[1] And now, what will be found in that day to be the portion of them that in this day do not come to God by Christ? None knows but God, with whom the reward of unbelievers is.

But writing and preaching is in vain as to such; let men say what they will, what they can, to persuade to come, to dissuade from neglecting to come, they are resolved not to stir. They will try if God will be so faithful to himself and to his Word, as to dare to condemn them to hell fire that have refused to hear and comply with the voice of him that speaketh from heaven.

But this is but a desperate venture. Several things declare that He is determined to be at a point in this matter—

1. The gallows are built—hell is prepared for the wicked.

2. There are those already in chains, and stand bound over to the judgment of that day, that are, as to creation, higher and greater than men, to wit, the angels that sinned.[2] Let sinners, then, look to themselves.

3. The Judge is prepared and appointed, and it hath fallen out to be HE that thou hast refused to come to God by; and that predicts no good to thee; for then will he say of all such, 'Those mine enemies, which would not that I should reign over them, bring hither, and slay *them* before me.'[3]

---

1 Psalm 50:3–4.

2 2 Peter 2:4.

3 Luke 19:27.

But what a surprise will it be to them that now have come to God by Christ to see themselves in heaven indeed, saved indeed, and possessed of everlasting life indeed. For alas! what is faith to possession? Faith that is mixed with many fears, that is opposed with many assaults, and that seems sometimes to be quite extinguished; I say, what is that to a seeing of myself in heaven? Hence it is said, that he shall then come to be admired in them that now believe, because they did here believe the testimony; then they shall admire that it was their lot to believe when they were in the world.[1] They shall also admire to think, to see, and behold, what believing has brought them to, while the rest, for refusing to come to God by Christ, drink their tears mixed with burning brimstone.

Repentance will not be found in heaven among them that come to God by Christ; no, hell is the place of untimely repentance; it is there where the tears will be mixed with gnashing of teeth, while they consider how mad, and worse, they were in not coming to God by Jesus Christ.

Then will their hearts and mouths be full of, 'Lord, Lord, open unto us.' But the answer will be, Ye shut me out of doors; 'I was a stranger, and ye took me not in;' besides, you refused to come to my Father by me, wherefore now you must go from my Father by me.[2]

They that will not be saved by Christ, must be damned by Christ; no man can escape one of the two. Refuse the first they may, but shun the second they cannot. And now they that would not come unto God by Christ will have leisure and time enough, if I may call it time, to consider what they have done in refusing to come to God by Christ. Now they will meditate warmly on this thing, now their thoughts will be burning hot about it, and it is too late, will be, in each thought, such a sting, that, like a bow of steel, it will continually strike him through.

Now they will bless those whom formerly they have despised, and commend those they once contemned. Now would the rich man

1 2 Thessalonians 1:10.
2 Matthew 25.

willingly change places with poor Lazarus, though he preferred his own condition before his in the world. The day of judgment will bring the worst to rights in their opinions; they will not be capable of misapprehending any more. They will never after that day put bitter for sweet, or darkness for light, or evil for good any more. Their madness will now be gone. Hell will be the unbeliever's bedlam house, and there God will tame them as to all those bedlam tricks and pranks which they played in this world, but not at all to their profit nor advantage; the gulf that God has placed and fixed betwixt heaven and hell will spoil all as to that.[1]

But what a joy will it be to the truly godly to think now that they are come to God by Christ! It was their mercy to begin to come, it was their happiness that they continued coming; but it is their glory that they are come, that they are come to God by Christ. To God! why, he is all! all that is good, essentially good, and eternally good. To God! the infinite ocean of good. To God, in friendly-wise, by the means of reconciliation; for the other now will be come to him to receive his anger, because they come not to him by Jesus Christ. Oh! that I could imagine; oh! that I could think, that I might write more effectually to thee of the happy estate of them that come to God by Christ.

But thus have I passed through the three former things, namely,

1. That of the intercession of Christ.

2. That of the benefit of intercession.

3. That of the persons that are interested in this intercession.

Wherefore now I come to the:

---

1 Luke 16:23–26.

CHAPTER IV

EVERY SINCERE COMER CERTAIN
OF SALVATION

FOURTH and last head, and that is, TO SHOW YOU THE CERTAIN-
TY OF THEIR REAPING THE BENEFIT OF HIS INTERCESSION.
'Wherefore he is able also to save them to the uttermost that come
unto God by him, seeing he ever liveth to make intercession for them.'

CHRIST EVER LIVING IS THE SAFETY OF COMERS

The certainty of their reaping the benefit of being saved that come
unto God by Christ is thus expressed: 'Seeing he ever liveth to make
intercession for them.' The intercession of Christ, and the lastingness
of it, is a sure token of the salvation of them that come unto God by
him.

Of his intercession, what it is, and for whom, we have spoken
already; of the success and prevalency of it, we have also spoken
before; but the reason of its successfulness of that we are to speak
now. And that reason, as the apostle suggesteth, lies in the continuance of it, 'Seeing he ever liveth to make intercession.' The apostle
also makes very much of the continuation of the priesthood of Christ
in other places of this epistle: he abides a priest continually, 'Thou *art*
a priest for ever.' He 'hath an unchangeable priesthood.'[1] And here he
'ever liveth to make intercession.'

Now, by the text is showed the reason why he so continually harpeth upon the durableness of it, namely, for that by the

1 Hebrews 7:3, 17, 21, 24.

unchangeableness of this priesthood we are saved; nay, saved demonstratively, apparently; it is evident we are. 'He is also able to save them to the uttermost that come unto God by him, seeing he ever liveth to make intercession for them.' For,

First, The durableness of his intercession proves that the covenant in which those who come to God by him are concerned and wrapt up is not shaken, broken, or made invalid by all their weaknesses and infirmities.

Christ is a priest according to covenant, and in all his acts of mediation he has regard to that covenant; so long as that covenant abides in its strength, so long Christ's intercession is of worth. Hence, when God cast the old high priest out of doors, he renders this reason for his so doing: 'Because they continued not in my covenant;' that is, neither priests nor people. Therefore were they cast out of the priesthood, and the people pulled down as to a church state.[1] Now, the covenant by which Christ acteth, as a priest, so far as we are concerned therein, he also himself acteth our part, being, indeed, the Head and Mediator of the body; wherefore, God doth not count that the covenant is broken, though we sin, if Christ Jesus our Lord is found to do by it what by law is required of us. Therefore he saith, 'If his children break my law, and keep not my commandments, I will visit their sins with a rod,' etc. But their sins shall not shake my covenant with my Beloved, nor cause that I for ever should reject them. 'My covenant will I not break, nor alter the thing that is gone out of my lips. His seed will I make to endure for ever, his seed shall endure for ever.'[2] Hence, it is clear that the covenant stands good to us as long as Christ stands good to God, or before his face; for he is not only our Mediator by covenant, but he himself is our conditions to God-ward; therefore he is said to be 'a covenant of the people,' or that which the holy God, by law, required of us.[3] Hence, again, he is said to be our justice or righteousness; to wit, which answereth to what is required

---

1 Hebrews 7:6–9.
2 Psalm 89:30–36.
3 Isaiah 42:6.

of us by the law. He is made unto us of God so, and in our room and in our stead presenteth himself to God. So, then, if any ask me by what Christ's priesthood is continued, I answer, by covenant; for that the covenant by which he is made priest abideth of full force. If any ask whether the church is concerned in that covenant, I answer, yes; yet so as that all points and parts thereof, that concern life and death everlasting, is laid upon his shoulders, and he alone is the doer of it. He is the Lord our righteousness, and he is the Saviour of the body, so that *my sins* break not the covenant; but *them*[1] notwithstanding, God's covenant stands fast with him, with him for evermore. And good reason, if no fault can be found with Christ, who is the person that did strike hands with his Father upon our account and for us; to wit, to do what was meet should be found upon us when we came to appear before God by him.

And that God himself doth so understand this matter is evident; because he also, by his own act, giveth and imputeth to us that good that we never did, that righteousness which we never wrought out; yea, and for the sake of that transmitteth our sins unto Christ, as to one that had not only well satisfied for them, but could carry them so far, both from us and from God, that they should never again come to be charged on the committers, to death and damnation.[2] The Scriptures are so plentiful for this, that he must be a Turk, or a Jew, or an atheist that denies it. Besides, God's commanding that men should believe in his Son unto righteousness well enough proveth this thing, and the reason of this command doth prove it with an over and above; to wit, 'For he hath made him *to be* sin for us, who knew no sin; that we might be made the righteousness of God in him.'[3] Hence comes out that proclamation from God, at the rising again of Christ from the dead: 'Be it known unto you, therefore, men *and* brethren, that through this man is preached unto you the forgiveness of sins;

---

1 'Them'—As Christ is the Saviour of both body and soul, notwithstanding the sins of the body, they break not the covenant; because it is God's covenant, and stands fast in Christ for evermore.—OFFOR.

2 Romans 4:1–5.

3 2 Corinthians 5:19–21.

and by him all that believe are justified from all things, from which ye could not be justified by the law of Moses.'[1]

If this be so, as indeed it is, then here lieth a great deal of this conclusion, 'he ever liveth to make intercession,' and of the demonstration of the certain salvation of him that cometh to God by him, 'seeing he ever liveth to make intercession for them.' For if Christ Jesus is a priest by covenant, and so abides as the covenant abides, and if, since the covenant is everlasting, his priesthood is unchangeable, then the man that cometh to God by him must needs be certainly saved; for if the covenant, the covenant of salvation, is not broken, none can show a reason why he that comes to Christ should be damned, or why the priesthood of Jesus Christ should cease. Hence, after the apostle had spoken of the excellency of his person and priesthood, he then shows that the benefit of the covenant of God remaineth with us, namely, that grace should be communicated unto us for his priesthood's sake, and that our sins and iniquities God would remember no more.[2] Now, as I also have already hinted, if this covenant, of which the Lord Jesus is Mediator and High Priest, has in the bowels of it, not only grace and remission of sins, but a promise that we shall be partakers thereof, through the blood of his priesthood, for so it comes to us; then, why should not we have boldness, not only to come to God by him, but to enter also 'into the holiest by the blood of Jesus, by that new and living way,' etc.

Second, But, further, this priesthood, as to the unchangeableness of it, is confirmed unto him 'with an oath, by him that said unto him, the Lord sware, and will not repent, Thou *art* a priest for ever.' This oath seems to me to be for the confirmation of the covenant, as it is worded before by Paul to the Galatians,[3] when he speaks of it with respect to that establishment that it also had on Christ's part by the sacrifice which he offered to God for us; yea, he then speaks of the mutual confirmation of it both by the Father and the Son. Now, I say,

---

1 Acts 13:38–39.
2 Hebrews 8:10–12; 10:16–22.
3 Galatians 3:15–17.

since, by this covenant he stands and abides a Priest, and since 'the Lord sware, and will not repent, saying, Thou *art* a priest for ever,' we are still further confirmed in the certain salvation of him that cometh to God by Christ.

The Lord, by swearing, confirmeth to Christ, and so to us in him, the immutability of his counsel,[1] and that he is utterly unchangeable in his resolutions 'to save them to the uttermost that come to God by Christ.' And this also shows that this covenant, and so the promise of remission of sins, is steadfast and immovable. And it is worth your noting the manner and nature of this oath, 'The Lord sware, and will not repent.' It is as much as to say, What I have now sworn I bind me for ever to stand to, or, I determine never to revoke; and that is, 'That thou art a priest for ever.' Now, as was said before, since his priesthood stands by covenant, and this covenant of his priesthood is confirmed by this oath, it cannot be but that he that comes by him to God must be accepted of him; for should such a one be rejected, it must be either for the greatness of his sins, or for want of merit in the sacrifice he presented and urged, as to the merit of it, before the mercy-seat. But let the reason specified be what it will, the consequence falls harder upon the sacrifice of Christ than it can do anywhere else, and so also upon the covenant, and at last upon God himself, who has sworn, and will not repent, that he is a Priest for ever. I thus discourse, to show you what dangerous conclusions follow from a conceit that some that come to God by Christ shall not be saved, though 'he ever liveth to make intercession for them.' And this I have further to say, that the Lord's swearing, since the manner of the oath is such as it is, and that it also tended to establish to Christ his priesthood to be unchangeable, it declareth that, as to the excellency of his sacrifice, he is eternally satisfied in the goodness and merit of it; and that he will never deny him anything that he shall ask for at his hands for his sufferings' sake. For this oath doth not only show God's firm resolution to keep his part of the covenant, in giving to Christ that which was covenanted for by him, but it declareth that,

---

1 Hebrews 6:16–18.

in the judgment of God, Christ's blood is able to save any sinner, and that he will never put stop nor check to his intercession, how great soever the sinners be that at any time he shall intercede for; so that the demonstration is clearer and clearer, 'He is able to save them to the uttermost that come unto God by him, seeing he ever liveth to make intercession for them.'

Third, This unchangeableness of the priesthood of Christ dependeth also upon his own life: 'This *man*, because he continueth ever, hath an unchangeable priesthood.'[1] Now although, perhaps, at first much may not appear in this text, yet the words that we are upon take their ground from them. 'This *man*, because he continueth ever, hath an unchangeable priesthood: wherefore he is able also'—that is, by his unchangeable priesthood—'to save them to the uttermost that come unto God by him, seeing he ever liveth to make intercession for them.'

The life of Christ, then, is a ground of the lastingness of his priesthood, and so a ground of the salvation of them that come unto God by him: 'We shall be saved by his life.'[2] Wherefore, in another place, this his life is spoken of with great emphasis—the power of an endless life. 'He is made (a priest), not after the law of a carnal commandment, but after the power of an endless life.'[3] An endless life is, then, a powerful thing; and indeed two things are very considerable in it—1. That it is above death, and so above him that hath the power of death, the devil. 2. In that it capacitates him to be the last in his own cause, and so to have the casting voice.

1. We will speak to the first, and for the better setting of it forth we will show what life it is of which the apostle here speaks; and then how, as to life, it comes to be so advantageous, both with respect to his office of priesthood and us.

What life is it that is thus the ground of his priesthood? It is a life taken, his own life rescued from the power of the grave; a life that we

1 Hebrews 7:24.
2 Romans 5:10.
3 Hebrews 7:16.

had forfeited, he being our surety; and a life that he recovered again, he being the Captain of our salvation: I lay down my life that I may take it again: 'this commandment have I received of my Father.'[1] It is a life, then, that was once laid down as the price of man's redemption, and a life won, gained, taken, or recovered again, as the token or true effect of the completing, by so dying, that redemption; wherefore it is said again, 'In that he died, he died unto sin once: but in that he liveth, he liveth unto God.'[2] He liveth as having pleased God by dying for our sins, as having merited his life by dying for our sins. Now if this life of his is a life merited and won by virtue of the death that he died, as Acts 2:24 doth clearly manifest; and if this life is the ground of the unchangeableness of this part of his priesthood, as we see it is, then it follows that this second part of his priesthood, which is called here intercession, is grounded upon the demonstrations of the virtue of his sacrifice, which is his life taken to live again; so, then, he holds this part of his priesthood, not by virtue of a carnal commandment, but by the power of an endless life; but by the power of a life rescued from death, and eternally exalted above all that any ways would yet assault it; for 'Christ being raised from the dead, dieth no more; death hath no more dominion over him.'[3] Hence Christ brings in his life, the life that he won to himself by his death, to comfort John withal when he fainted under the view of that overcoming glory that he saw upon Christ in his vision of him at Patmos: 'And he laid his right hand upon me,' said he, 'saying unto me, Fear not; I am the first and the last: I *am* he that liveth and was dead, and, behold, I am alive for evermore. Amen.'[4] Why should Christ bring in his life to comfort John, if it was not a life advantageous to him? But the advantageousness of it doth lie not merely in the being of life, but in that it was a life laid down for his sins, and a life taken up again for his justification; a life lost to ransom him, and a life won to save him; as also the text affirmeth, saying, 'He is able to save to the uttermost

1 John 10:18.
2 Romans 6:10.
3 Romans 6:9.
4 Revelation 1:17–18.

them that come unto God by him, seeing he ever liveth to make intercession for them.'

Again; it is yet more manifest that Christ receiving of his life again was the death and destruction of the enemy of his people; and to manifest that it was so, therefore he adds (after he had said, 'And, behold, I am alive for evermore. Amen'), 'And I have the keys of hell and of death.' I have the power over them; I have them under me; I tread them down by being a victor, a conqueror, and one that has got the dominion of life (for he now is the Prince of life), one that lives for evermore. Amen. Hence it is said again, He 'hath abolished death, and brought life and immortality to light through the gospel.'[1] He hath abolished death by his death (by death he destroyed him that had the power of death, that is, the devil), and brought life (a very emphatical expression); and brought it from whence? From God, who raised him from the dead; and brought it to light, to our view and sight, by the word of the truth of the gospel.

So, then, the life that he now hath is a life once laid down as the price of our redemption; a life obtained and taken to him again as the effect of the merit that was in the laying down thereof; a life by the virtue of which death, and sin, and the curse is overcome; and so a life that is above them for ever. This is the life that he liveth—to wit, this meriting, purchasing, victorious life—and that he improveth while he ever so lives to make intercession for us.

This life, then, is a continual plea and argument with God for them that come to him by Christ, should he make no other intercession, but only show to God that he liveth; because his thus living saith, that he has satisfied for the sins of them that come unto God by him. It testifies, moreover, that those—to wit, death, the grave, and hell—are overcome by him for them; because indeed he liveth, and hath their keys. But now, add to life, to a life meritorious, intercession, or an urging of this meritorious life by way of prayer for his, and against all those that seek to destroy them, since they themselves also have been already overcome by his death, and what an encouraging

1 2 Timothy 1:10.

consideration is here for all them that come to God by him, to hope
for life eternal. But,

2. Let us speak a word to the second head—namely, for that his
living for ever capacitates him to be the last in his own cause, and
to have the casting voice, and that is an advantage next to what is
chiefest.

His cause; what is his cause? but that the death that he died when
he was in the world was and is of merit sufficient to secure all those
from hell, or, as the text has it, to save them that come unto God by
him, to save them to the uttermost. Now, if this cause be faulty, why
doth he live? yea, he liveth by the power of God, by the power of God
towards us; or with a respect to our welfare, for he liveth to make
intercession, intercession against Satan our accuser, for us.[1] Besides,
he liveth before God, and to God, and that after he had given his life
a ransom for us. What can follow more clearly from this, but that
amends were made by him for those souls for whose sins he suffered
upon the tree? Wherefore, since his Father has given him his life and
favour, and that after he died for our sins, it cannot be thought but
that the life he now liveth, is a life that he received as the effect of the
merit of his passion for us.

God is just, and yet Christ liveth, and yet Christ liveth in heaven!
God is just, and yet Christ our passover liveth there, do what our foes
can to the contrary!

And this note, by the way, that though the design of Satan against
us, in his labouring continually to accuse us to God, and to prevail
against our salvation, seems to terminate here, yet indeed it is also
laid against the very life of Christ, and that his priesthood might
be utterly overthrown; and, in conclusion, that God also might be
found unjust in receiving of such whose sins have not been satisfied
for, and so whose souls are yet under the power of the devil. For he
that objects against him for whom Christ intercedes, objects against
Christ and his merits; and he that objects against Christ's intercession, objects against God, who has made him a priest for ever. Behold

1 2 Corinthians 13:4.

you, therefore, how the cause of God, of Christ, and of the souls that come to God by him are interwoven; they are all wrapt up in one bottom. Mischief one, and you mischief all; overthrow that soul, and you overthrow his intercessor; and overthrow him, and you overthrow even him that made him a priest for ever. For the text is without restriction: 'He is able to save to the uttermost them, that come unto God by him.' He saith not, now and then one, or sinners of an inferior rank in sin, but them that come to God by him, how great soever their transgressions are, as is clear in that it addeth this clause, 'to the uttermost.' 'He is able to save them to the uttermost.' But if he were not, why did the King send, yea, come and loose him, and let him go free; yea, admit him into his presence; yea, make him Lord over all his people, and deliver all things into his hand?

But he liveth, he ever liveth, and is admitted to make intercession, yea, is ordained of God so to do; therefore he is 'able to save to the uttermost them that come unto God by him.' This, therefore, that he liveth, seeing he liveth to God and his judgment, and in justice is made so to do, it is chiefly with reference to his life as Mediator for their sakes for whom he makes intercession. He liveth to make intercession. And in that it is said he liveth ever, what is it but that he must live, and outlive all his enemies; for he must live, yea, reign, till all his enemies are put under his feet.[1] Yea, his very intercessions must live till they are all dead and gone. For the devil and sin must not live for ever, not for ever to accuse. Time is coming when due course of law will have an end, and all cavillers will be cast over the bar. But then and after that, Christ our high priest shall live, and so shall his intercessions; yea, and also all them for whom he makes intercession, seeing they come unto God by him.

Now if he lives, and outlives all, and if his intercession has the casting voice, since also he pleadeth in his prayers a sufficient merit before a just God, against a lying, malicious, clamorous, and envious adversary, he must needs carry the cause, the cause for himself and his people, to the glory of God and their salvation. So, then, his life

1 1 Corinthians 15:25.

and intercession must prevail, there can be no withstanding of it. Is not this, then, a demonstration clear as the sun, that they that come to God by him shall be saved, seeing he ever liveth to make intercession for them?

Fourth, The duration of Christ's intercession, as it is grounded upon a covenant betwixt God and him, upon an oath also, and upon his life, so it is grounded upon the validity of his merits. This has been promiscuously touched before, but since it is an essential to the lastingness of his intercession, it will be to the purpose to lay it down by itself.

Intercession, then, I mean Christ's intercession, is, that those for whom he died with full intention to save them, might be brought into that inheritance which he hath purchased for them. Now, then, his intercession must, as to length and breadth, reach no further than his merits, for he may not pray for those for whom he died not. Indeed, if we take in the utmost extent of his death, then we must beware, for his death is sufficient to save the whole world. But his intercessions are kept within a narrower compass. The altar of burnt-offerings was a great deal bigger than the altar of incense, which was a figure of Christ's intercession.[1] But this, I say, his intercession is for those for whom he died with full intention to save them; wherefore it must be grounded upon the validity of his sufferings. And, indeed, his intercession is nothing else, that I know of, but a presenting of what he did in the world for us unto God, and pressing the value of it for our salvation. The blood of sprinkling is that which speaketh meritoriously,[2] it is by the value of that that God measureth out and giveth unto us grace and life eternal; wherefore Christ's intercessions also must be ordered and governed by merit: 'By his own blood he entered into the holy place, having (before by it) obtained eternal redemption for us,' for our souls.[3]

Now, if by blood he entered in thither, by blood he must also

---

1 Exodus 27:1; 30:1; Revelation 8:3.
2 Hebrews 12:24.
3 Hebrews 9:12.

make intercession there. His blood made way for his entrance thither, his blood must make way for our entrance thither. Though here, again, we must beware; for his blood did make way for him as Priest to intercede; his blood makes way for us, as for those redeemed by it, that we might be saved. This, then, shows sufficiently the worth of the blood of Christ, even his ever living to make intercession for us; for the merit of his blood lasts all the while that he doth, and for all them for whom he ever liveth to make intercession. Oh, precious blood! oh, lasting merit!

Blood must be pleaded in Christ's intercession, because of justice, and to stop the mouth of the enemy, and also to encourage us to come to God by him. Justice, since that is of the essence of God, must concur in the salvation of the sinner; but how can that be, since it is said at first, 'In the day thou eatest thereof, thou shalt surely die,' unless a plenary[1] satisfaction be made for sin to the pleasing of the mighty God. The enemy also would else never let go his objecting against our salvation. But now God has declared that our salvation is grounded on justice, because merited by blood. And though God needed not to have given his Son to die for us that he might save us, and stop the mouth of the devil in so doing, yet this way of salvation has done both, and so it is declared, we are 'justified freely by his grace, through the redemption that is in Christ Jesus: whom God hath set forth *to be* a propitiation through faith in his blood, to declare his righteousness for the remission of sins that are past . . . to declare, *I say*, at this time his righteousness: that he might be just, and the justifier of him which believeth in Jesus.'[2] So, then, here is also a ground of intercession, even the blood shed for us before.

And that you may see it yet more for your comfort, God did, at Christ's resurrection, to show what a price he set upon his blood, bid him ask of him the heathen, and he would give him the uttermost parts of the earth for his possession.[3] His blood, then, has value

---

1 Plenary—full, perfect, or complete.—Offor.
2 Romans 3:24–25.
3 Psalm 2:8.

enough in it to ground intercession upon; yea, there is more worth in it than Christ will plead or improve for men by way of intercession. I do not at all doubt but that there is virtue enough in the blood of Christ, would God Almighty so apply it, to save the souls of the whole world. But it is the blood of Christ, his own blood; and he may do what he will with his own. It is also the blood of God, and he also may restrain its merits, or apply it as he sees good. But the coming soul, he shall find and feel the virtue thereof, even the soul that comes to God by Christ; for he is the man concerned in its worth, and he ever liveth to make intercession for him. Now, seeing the intercession of Christ is grounded upon a covenant, an oath, a life, and also upon the validity of his merits, it must of necessity be prevalent, and so drive down all opposition before it. This, therefore, is the last part of the text, and that which demonstrateth that he that comes to God by Christ shall be saved, seeing 'he ever liveth to make intercession for him.'

I have now done what I intend upon this subject when I have drawn a few inferences from this also.

INFERENCES FROM THE CERTAINTY OF BENEFIT FROM CHRIST'S INTERCESSION

First, then, hence I infer that *the souls saved by Christ are in themselves in a most deplorable condition.* Oh, what ado, as I may say, is here before one sinner can be eternally saved! Christ must die; but that is not all; the Spirit of grace must be given to us; but that is not all;—but Christ must also ever live to make intercession for us. And as he doth this for all, so he doth it for each one. He interceded for me, before I was born, that I might in time, at the set time, come into being. After that, he also made intercession for me, that I might be kept from hell in the time of my unregenerate state, until the time of my call and conversion. Yet again, he then intercedes that the work now begun in my soul may be perfected, not only to the day of my dissolution, but unto the day of Christ; that is, until he comes to judgment.[1] So that, as he began to save me before I had being, so he will go on to save me when I am dead and gone, and will never leave off to save me until he has set me before his face for ever.

But, I say, what a deplorable condition has our sin put us into, that there must be all this ado to save us. Oh, how hardly is sin got out of the soul when once it is in! Blood takes away the guilt; inherent grace weakens the filth; but the *grave* is the place, at the mouth of which, sin, as to the being of sin, and the saved, must have a perfect and final parting.[2] Not that the grave of itself is of a sin-purging quality, but God will follow Satan home to his own door; for the grave is the door or gate of hell, and will there, where the devil thought to have swallowed us up, even there by the power of his mercy make us, at our coming thence, shine like the sun, and look like angels. Christ, all this while, ever liveth to make intercession for us.

Second, Hence, also, I infer that *as Satan thought he struck home at first, when he polluted our nature, and brought our souls to death, so he is marvellous loath to lose us, and to suffer his lawful captives now to escape his hands.* He is full of fire against us, full of the fire of malice, as is manifest—

1. Not only by his first attempt upon our first parents, but behold, when the Deliverer came into the world, how he roared. He sought his death while he was an infant; he hated him in his cradle; he persecuted him while he was but a bud and blossom.[3] When he was come to riper years, and began to manifest his glory, yet, lest the world should be taken with him, how politicly did this old serpent, called the Devil and Satan, work? He possessed people that he had a devil, and was mad, and a deceiver; that he wrought his miracles by magic art and by the devil; that the prophets spake nothing of him, and that he sought to overthrow the government which was God's ordinance. And, not being contented with all this, he pursued him to the death, and could never rest until he had spilt his blood upon the ground like water. Yea,

---

1 Philippians 1:6.
2 Isaiah 38:10.
3 Matthew 2.

so insatiable was his malice, that he set the soldiers to forge lies about him to the denial of his resurrection, and so managed that matter that what they said has become a stumbling-block to the Jews to this very day.[1]

2. When he was ascended to God, and so was out of his reach, yet how busily went he about to make war with his people.[2] Yea, what horrors and terrors, what troubles and temptations, has God's church met with from that day till now! Nor is he content with persecutions and general troubles; but oh! how doth he haunt the spirits of the Christians with blasphemies and troubles, with darkness and frightful fears; sometimes to their distraction, and often to the filling the church with outcries.

3. Yet his malice is in the pursuit, and now his boldness will try what it can do with God, either to tempt him to reject his Son's mediation, or to reject them that come to God by him for mercy. And this is one cause among many why 'he ever liveth to make intercession for them that come to God by him.'

4. And if he cannot overthrow, if he knows he cannot overthrow them, yet he cannot forbear but vex and perplex them, even as he did their Lord, from the day of their conversion to the day of their ascension to glory.

Third, Hence I infer that *the love of Christ to his, is an unwearied love, and it must needs be so; an undaunted love, and it must needs be so.* Who but Jesus Christ would have undertaken such a task as the salvation of the sinner is, if Jesus Christ had passed us by? It is true which is written of him, 'He shall not fail, nor be discouraged, till he have set judgment in the earth,' etc. If he had not set his 'face like a flint,' the greatness of this work would surely have daunted his mind.[3]

For do but consider what sin is from which they must be saved; do but consider what the devil and the curse is from which they must

1 John 10:20; 7:12; Matthew 9:34; John 7:52; Luke 23:2; Matthew 28:11–15.
2 Revelation 12.
3 Isaiah 42:4; 50:6–7.

be saved; and it will easily be concluded by you that it is he that full rightly deserveth to have his name called Wonderful, and his love such as verily passeth knowledge.

Consider, again, by what means these souls are saved, even with the loss of his life, and, together with it, the loss of the light of his Father's face. I pass by here and forbear to speak of the matchless contradiction of sinners which he endured against himself, which could not but be a great grief, or, as himself doth word it, a breaking of heart unto him; but all this did not, could not, hinder.

Join to all this, his everlasting intercession for us, and the effectual management thereof with God for us; and, withal, the infinite number of times that we by sin provoke him to spue us out of his mouth, instead of interceding for us, and the many times also that his intercession is repeated by the repeating of our faults, and this love still passes knowledge, and is by us to be wondered at. What did, or what doth, the Lord Jesus see in us to be at all this care, and pains, and cost to save us? What will he get of us by the bargain but a small pittance of thanks and love? for so it is, and ever will be, when compared with his matchless and unspeakable love and kindness towards us.

Oh, how unworthy are we of this love! How little do we think of it! But, most of all, the angels may be astonished to see how little we are affected with that of which we pretend to know. But neither can this prevail with him to put us out of the scroll in which all the names of them are written for whom he doth make intercession to God. Let us cry, Grace, grace unto it.

Fourth, Hence again I infer that *they shall be saved that come to God by Christ, when the devil and sin have done what they can to hinder it.* This is clear, for that the strife is now, who shall be lord of all, whether Satan, the prince of this world, or Christ Jesus, the Son of God; or which can lay the best claim to God's elect, he that produceth their sins against them, or he that laid down his heart's blood a price of redemption for them. Who, then, shall condemn when Christ has died, and doth also make intercession? Stand still, angels, and behold how the Father divideth his Son 'a portion with the great;' and how he divideth 'the spoil with the strong: because he hath poured out his soul unto death, and was numbered with the transgressors, and bare the sin of many, and made intercession for the transgressors.'[1] The grace of God and blood of Christ will, before the end of the world, make brave work among the sons of men! They shall come to a wonderment to God by Christ, and be saved by a wonderment for Christ's sake—'Behold these shall come from far: and lo, these from the north and from the west, and these from the land of Sinim.'[2]

Behold, these, and these, and these shall come, and lo, these, and these, and these from the land of Sinim! This is to denote the abundance that shall come in to God by Christ towards the latter end of the world—namely, when Antichrist is gone to bed in the sides of the pit's mouth; then shall nations come in and be saved, and shall walk in the light of the Lord.[3] But, I say, what encouragement would there be for sinners thus to do if that the Lord Jesus by his intercession were not able to save 'even to the uttermost' them that come unto God by him.

Fifth, Hence again I infer that *here is ground for confidence to them that come to God by Christ.* Confidence to the end becomes us who have such a High Priest, such an Intercessor as Jesus Christ; who would dishonour such a Jesus by doubting that, that all the devils in hell cannot discourage by all their wiles? He is a tried stone, he is a sure foundation; a man may confidently venture his soul in his hand, and not fear but he will bring him safe home. Ability, love to the person, and faithfulness to trust committed to him, will do all; and all these are with infinite fullness in him. He has been a Saviour these four thousand years already—two thousand before the law, two thousand in the time of the law—besides the sixteen hundred years

---

1 Isaiah 53:12.

2 Isaiah 49:12.

3 Bunyan saw that time very far off, which much more nearly approaches us: when Antichrist, and the interference of the civil power, under his influence, with matters of faith and worship, will find a grave in the side of the pit's mouth; when no national barriers, either Pagan, Popish, or Protestant, shall exist to prevent the glorious spread of pure and vital Christianity. However abundant that harvest of souls shall be, there will prove a superabundance of grace in Christ to supply all their wants.—OFFOR.

he has in his flesh continued to make intercession for them that come unto God by him. Yet the day is to come, yea, will never come, that he can be charged with any fault, or neglect of the salvation of any of them that at any time have come unto God by him. What ground, then, is here for confidence that Christ will make a good end with me, since I come unto God by him, and since he ever liveth to make intercession for me. Let me, then, honour him, I say, by setting on his head the crown of his undertakings for me, by the believing that he is able to save me 'even to the uttermost, seeing he ever liveth to make intercession for me.'

Sixth, Hence also I infer that *Christ ought to bear and wear the glory of our salvation for ever.* He has done it, he has wrought it out. 'Give unto the Lord, O ye kindreds of the people, give unto the Lord glory and strength.' Do not sacrifice to your own inventions, do not give glory to the work of your own hands. Your reformations, your works, your good deeds, and all the glory of your doing, cast them at the feet of this High Priest, and confess that glory belongs unto him—'Worthy is the Lamb that was slain, to receive power, and riches, and wisdom, and strength, and honour, and glory, and blessing.'[1] 'And they shall hang upon him all the glory of his Father's house, the offspring and the issue, all vessels of small quantity, from the vessels of cups, even to all the vessels of flagons.'[2] Oh! the work of our redemption by Christ is such as wanteth not provocation to us to bless, and praise, and glorify Jesus Christ. Saints, set to the work and glorify him in your body and in your souls; him who has bought us with a price, and glorify God and the Father by him.[3]

---

1 Revelation 5:12.
2 Isaiah 22:24.
3 1 Corinthians 6:20.

THE USE

I COME now to make some use of this discourse; and,

Use First, Let me exhort you to the study of this, as of other the truths of our Lord Jesus Christ. The priestly office of Christ is the first and great thing that is presented to us in the gospel— namely, how that he died for our sins, and gave himself to the cross, that the blessing of Abraham might come upon us through him.[1] But now because this priestly office of his is divided into two parts, and because one of them—to wit, this of his intercession—is to be accomplished for us within the veil, therefore, as we say among men, out of sight out of mind, he is too much as to this forgotten by us. We satisfy ourselves with the slaying of the sacrifice; we look not enough after our Aaron as he goes into the holiest, there to sprinkle the mercy-seat with blood upon our account. God forbid that the least syllable of what I say should be intended by me, or construed by others, as if I sought to diminish the price paid by Christ for our redemption in this world. But since his dying is his laying down his price, and his intercession the urging and managing the worthiness of it in the presence of God against Satan, there is glory to be found therein, and we should look after him into the holy place. The second part of the work of the high priests under the law, had great glory and sanctity put upon it; forasmuch as the holy garments were provided for him to officiate in within the veil, also it was there that the altar stood on which he offered incense; also there was the mercy-seat and

---

1 1 Corinthians 15:1–6; Galatians 3:13–16.

the cherubims of glory, which were figures of the angels, that love to be continually looking and prying into the management of this second part of the priesthood of Christ in the presence of God; for although themselves are not the persons so immediately concerned therein as we, yet the management of it, I say, is with so much grace, and glory, and wisdom, and effectualness, that it is a heaven to the angels to see it. Oh! to enjoy the odorous scent, and sweet memorial, the heart-refreshing perfumes, that ascend continually from the mercy-seat to the 'above' where God is; and also to behold how effectual it is to the end for which it is designed, is glorious; and he that is not somewhat let into this by the grace of God, there is a great thing lacking to his faith, and he misseth of many a sweet bit that he might otherwise enjoy. Wherefore, I say, be exhorted to the study of this part of Christ's work in the managing of our salvation for us. And the ceremonies of the law may be a great help to you as to this, for though they be out of use now as to practice, yet the signification of them is rich, and that from which many gospellers[1] have got much. Wherefore I advise that you read the five books of Moses often; yea, read, and read again, and do not despair of help to understand something of the will and mind of God therein, though you think they are fast locked up from you. Neither trouble your heads though you have not commentaries and expositions; pray and read, and read and pray; for a little from God is better than a great deal from men. Also, what is from men is uncertain, and is often lost and tumbled over and over by men; but what is from God is fixed as a nail in a sure place. I know there are [peculiar] times of temptation, but I speak now as to the common course of Christianity. There is nothing that so abides with us as what we receive from God; and the reason why Christians at this day are at such a loss as to some things is, because they are content with what comes from men's mouths, without searching and kneeling before God, to know of him the

---

1 Gospellers—a nickname given to the Reformers, when first a holy band determined, at the imminent risk of life, to read the New Testament or Gospels in English. It was like the term Methodist, a few years ago. The gospel has now so much spread, that these terms of reproach are only used by fanatics.—OFFOR.

truth of things. Things that we receive at God's hand come to us as things from the *minting house*, though old in themselves, yet new to us. Old truths are always new to us if they come to us with the smell of heaven upon them. I speak not this because I would have people despise their ministers, but to show that there is nowadays so much idleness among professors as hinders them from a diligent search after things, and makes them take up short of that that is sealed by the Spirit of testimony to the conscience. Witness the great decays at this day amongst us, and that strange revolting from truth once professed by us.

USE SECOND, As I would press you to an earnest study and search after this great truth, so I would press you to a diligent improvement of it to yourselves and to others. To know truth for knowledge' sake is short of a gracious disposition of soul; and to communicate truth out of a desire of praise and vain-glory for so doing is also a swerving from godly simplicity; but to improve what I know for the good of myself and others is true Christianity indeed. Now truths received may be improved with respect to myself and others, and that several ways—

1. To myself, when I search after the power that belongs to those notions that I have received of truth. There belongs to every true notion of truth a power; the notion is the shell—the power is the kernel and life. Without this last, truth doth me no good, nor those to whom I communicate it. Hence Paul said to the Corinthians, 'When I come to you again, I will know not the speech of them that are puffed up, but the power. For the kingdom of God *is* not in word, but in power.'[1] Search, then, after the power of what thou knowest, for it is the power that will do thee good. Now this will not be got but by earnest prayer, and much attending upon God; also there must not be admitted by thee that thy heart be stuffed with cumbering cares of this world, for they are of a choking nature.

Take heed of slighting that little that thou hast; a good improvement of little is the way to make that little thrive, and the way to obtain additions thereto: 'He that is faithful in that which is least is

---

1 1 Corinthians 4:19–20.

faithful also in much; and he that is unjust in the least is unjust also in much.'[1]

2. Improve them to others, and that, (1.) By labouring to instill them upon their hearts by good and wholesome words, presenting all to them with the authority of the Scriptures. (2.) Labour to enforce those instillings on them by showing them by thy life the peace, the glorious effects that they have upon thy soul.

Lastly, Let this doctrine give thee boldness to come to God. Shall Jesus Christ be interceding in heaven? Oh, then, be thou a praying man on earth; yea, take courage to pray. Think thus with thyself—I go to God, to God, before whose throne the Lord Jesus is ready to hand my petitions to him; yea, 'he ever lives to make intercession for me.' This is a great encouragement to come to God by prayers and supplications for ourselves, and by intercessions for our families, our neighbours, and enemies. Farewell.

---

1 Luke 16:10.

Made in the USA
Las Vegas, NV
02 November 2023

80121909R00069